First published in 2013 by:
Zega Enterprises
Pottsville, New South Wales, Australia
zega.enterprises@live.com.au

The Complete Cockroach Breeding Manual
Edition 1: August 2013
Author: Glenn Kvassay
ISBN: 978-0-9873062-3-4 (pbk)

© Glenn Kvassay 2013
© Photographs, diagrams, tables: by Glenn Kvassay or as credited 2013

All rights reserved. No part of this publication may be reproduced, stored in a retrieval system, or transmitted, in any form or by any means, electronic, mechanical, photocopying, recording, duplicating or otherwise, without the prior written permission of the author. The methods contained in this manual (containers or individual components) may not be manufactured and sold without the written consent from the author. Please contact Glenn Kvassay for all permission requests, or if are aware of any breaches of copyright at zega.enterprises@live.com.au.

Techniques, materials, personal skill level and site conditions vary widely between individuals, which may alter outcomes described in this book. The author takes no responsibility for any liability of damages, actions, loss or injury resulting from the use of information in this book.

Always follow manufacture's operating instructions and observe safety precautions when using equipment/tools and/or materials described in this book. If in any doubt as to the correct or safe procedure to follow for any activity described, seek professional advice.

We thank you for your purchase and we hope your animals enjoy the benefits of a fresh and plentiful supply of cockroaches. This manual has been developed following many years of trial and error by the author to provide you with the best techniques and methods for successful cricket breeding. If you have not purchased this manual or have inadvertently received a copy, please support the work of the author, and the development of additional techniques for wildlife enthusiasts and purchase it from www.zegaenterprises.com.au.

THE COMPLETE COCKROACH BREEDING MANUAL

                                                                                                      Page

Foreword 4

1.0   Introduction

1.1   Benefits of Breeding Cockroaches 6
1.2   How to Use This Manual 8
1.3   Conversions 10

2.0   Cockroach Biology

2.1   Anatomy 11
2.2   Biology and Behaviour 12
2.3   Species Selection 14

3.0   Container Design and Construction

3.1   Choosing a Container 17
3.2   Lids 18
3.3   Ventilation 18
3.4   Feeding Port 19
3.5   Screening 20
3.6   Barrier Cream 20
3.7   Component Set-up 20
3.8   Making a Container 21

4.0   Breeding

4.1   Breeding Overview 27
4.2   Zega Cockroach Breeding System 27

5.0   Food and Water Requirements

5.1   Food and Water Components 32
5.2   Dry Food- Nutrition and Processing 33
5.3   Wet Food- Nutrition and Processing 36
5.4   Gut Loading and Dusting 38
5.5   Feeding Cockroaches to Animals 39

6.0   Making Food and Water Dispensers

6.1   Design Considerations for Food and Water Dispensers 46
6.2   Food Dispenser- Small Scale Production 47
6.3   Food Dispenser- Large Scale Production 48

7.0 Heating and Storage

7.1 Heating and Humidity Requirements 61
7.2 Heating Systems 62
7.3 Reducing Heating Costs 65
7.4 Estimating Heating Costs 67
7.5 Managing Excessive Heat 68
7.6 Storage of Colony 68

8.0 Maintenance and Pest Management

8.1 Maintenance 70
8.2 Cleaning 71
8.3 Pests 79
8.4 Genetics 82
8.5 Safety 83

9.0 Grading and Selling

9.1 Grading by Size 84
9.2 Estimating the Number of Cockroaches 87
9.3 Packaging and Transport 91
9.4 Economics 93
9.5 Marketing 96
9.6 Record Keeping 97

Glossary 100

List of Tables

Table 1- Advantages and Disadvantages between Breeding Cockroaches and Crickets 7
Table 2- Conversion between Imperial and Metric Units 10
Table 3- Overview of Constructing a Container- Efficient Method 22
Table 4- Detailed Instructions for Constructing a Container- Efficient Method 24
Table 5- How to Make a Zega Cockroach Breeding System 29
Table 6- Nutritional Comparison between Different Dry Food Types 34
Table 7- How to Make a Small Scale Food Dispenser 47
Table 8- Making a Food Tray 49
Table 9- Making a Large Scale Food Disperser 50
Table 10- Making a Large Scale Water Dispenser 55
Table 11- Making a Large Scale Water Dispenser with Pebbles 59
Table 12- Temperature Ranges for Cockroaches 61
Table 13- Maintenance Schedule 70
Table 14- Cleaning Food and Water Dispensers 72
Table 15- Removing Detritus 75
Table 16- Making an Ant Guard for Power Cords 80
Table 17- Grading Cockroaches 84
Table 18- Counting Cockroaches- Large Scale 88
Table 19- Transport Methods 91

List of Diagrams and Figures

Diagram 2.1	Anatomy of a Cockroach- Top View	11
Diagram 2.2	Anatomy of a Cockroach- Bottom View	11
Figure 3.3	Air Flow through a Container	18
Figure 4.1	Diagrammatic Representation of a "Zega Cockroach Breeding System"	28

Appendixes

Appendix 1	Example Marketing Brochure	102

FOREWORD

From a young age I had a fascination with wildlife, especially reptiles and insectivorous animals. This curiosity led me to become a biologist and to have a passion for keeping and breeding native wildlife. I started breeding cockroaches to reduce my expenses at the pet store associated with wildlife rescue and reptile keeping.

1.1 Northern Quoll *(Dasyurus hallucatus)*

For example, one of my passions is rehabilitating injured or orphaned marsupial carnivores called Quolls (Australia's native cat- Refer to photo 1.1). Luke Jackson and I established the Far North Quoll Seekers Network (FNQSN) in northern Australia (*http://www.wildlife.org.au/*), to conserve quolls which are in threat of extinction. Quolls have an insatiable appetite for live foods, with a single animal eating a pet bought container of cockroaches every second day. It quickly became apparent that keeping a family of Quolls over a period of many months was an expensive exercise.

To add to my hip pocket woes, were a growing number of pet monitor and dragon lizards. Like most people in today's busy lifestyle I didn't have the time to scrummage through the garden looking for insects…..and then there's the potential risk of pesticides! The solution was to breed cockroaches and cockroaches myself. The only problem was that I had a full time job, a young family and not nearly enough time to breed cockroaches and crickets in the way described in brief and incomplete internet blogs. Over time I developed techniques which greatly streamlined the process and now breeding cockroaches can be done with half the maintenance and hassle, and crickets can be kept with around the same amount of effort as cockroaches. After a while it became apparent that many people require a regular and fresh supply of live foods and I was soon being approached by wildlife parks, pet stores, wildlife rescue members, vets and the general public. This led me to breed them on a small to medium scale for many years and to a wide range of clients.

Breeding cockroaches is an ongoing experiment to find better and more efficient methods. If you have tips or experiences to share, please do not hesitate to pass on this information, for the benefit of all reptile and wildlife enthusiasts. Above all have fun, and I hope you and your animals enjoy a productive and successful breeding cockroach colony!

Glenn Kvassay
Bachelor of Applied Science (Biology)

1.0 INTRODUCTION

A plentiful and fresh supply of live food is the cornerstone of keeping healthy and happy insectivorous animals. Many of you will know the thrill of providing live food to your animals, and seeing how they benefit both physically and mentally. Sadly for the consumer, purchasing cockroaches from a pet store is expensive and often results in the disappointing experience of purchasing dead or dying cockroaches. Many people attempt to breed cockroaches and crickets but often fail over the long term, due to the demanding maintenance required by conventional methods. With the systems and techniques contained in this manual you will be able to produce large amounts of cockroaches inexpensively, consistently and with minimal effort. This manual containers step by step instructions in conjunction with over 145 photos, tables and diagrams make the process easy.

1.2 The greatest benefit of breeding cockroaches is a healthy animal and a happy owner!!

This manual will benefit people who wish to:

- Reduce costs associated with providing live food for insectivorous animals such as reptiles, frogs, arachnids (spiders, scorpions) and fish.
- Produce an additional income by selling directly to the general public, pet stores and wildlife parks etc.
- Wildlife rescue carers who require large quantities of cockroaches to feed insectivorous mammals, birds, reptiles and amphibians.
- Wildlife carer groups that wish to raise money and provide inexpensive feeder cockroaches for their members or as a fund raiser.
- Pet stores/wildlife parks and zoos which wish to breed cockroaches to reduce operating costs.
- Cockroaches and crickets are now found in gourmet restaurants and are bred as mainstream food source in Asia.
- University and research institutes
- Fishermen

Cockroaches are prolific breeders which lend themselves to being bred for commercial production. With a little extra effort, you may wish to add extra containers and sell excess stock to the public and turn an expense into an income. In developing this manual a number of options are provided from simple set ups suitable for small collections to more elaborate systems suitable for commercial production.

Below is a summary of the information contained in this manual:

- Systems which minimise maintenance in conjunction with automated feeding/watering devices.
- Efficient container design, which is durable, maximises growth rates, and saves time in maintenance and feeding activities.
- Breeding methods that allow cockroaches to be breed with significantly less maintenance, fewer escapees and without offensive odours.
- Plenty of tips on how to save time, effort and money through energy conservation or efficient food storage and processing.
- Details how to manage a commercial colony from breeding through to dispatch, transport and marketing.
- Plenty of tips to make the dispatch of cockroaches to your animals with minimal effort.

This manual is an accumulation of years of experience and experimentation which will provide you with a short cut to successful cockroach breeding.

1.1 Benefits of Breeding Cockroaches

The hit and miss quality of store bought animals means it is not only expensive, but it prevents many people from keeping insectivorous animals. One of the greatest benefits of breeding your own cockroaches is an unlimited supply of live foods, which are in good condition.

Cockroaches are a nutritionally rich source of proteins (comprising of many essential amino acids), carbohydrates, fats, minerals and water for your animals. They are easily digested and provide good roughage for your animals. Apart from the obvious nutritional benefits of cockroaches, they also play an important role in stimulating an animal's natural hunting instincts and quality of life.

As detailed in Section 9.4 (Economics) substantial savings can be made from producing your own cockroaches. For instance feeding a single adult bearded dragon can cost around $730 per annum (Australian costing). The waste wet food generated from an average family (two adults, two kids) can produce sufficient cockroaches to support between two to four adult bearded dragons (depending on cricket consumption rate chosen) which represent a financial outlay of approximately $1456 per annum. The savings mount up the more wildlife you keep, which seems to be an occupational hazard for wildlife and reptile enthusiasts! Many reptile enthusiasts/wildlife parks spend many thousands of dollars each year feeding insectivorous animals.

Other people may wish to breed cockroaches for profit. With a little extra effort, people can add extra containers and sell excess stock to the public. Many wildlife and reptile enthusiasts are always looking for a cheap and fresh supply of food for their animals. This is a great way to turn an expense into an income. If you have unused space in your house or unused shed areas, why not use this area to produce a regular income. I have found that with a motto "More Cockroaches for Less Money" customers will quickly find you.

1.0- Introduction

You may be surprised to learn that many pet stores and wildlife parks prefer a local supplier as they generally have a lower death rate, are better quality product (reduced or minimal travel times), have longer shelf life and are cheaper as they do not need to pay for expensive air freight (which can be just as expensive as the cockroach order). Having a local breeder provides them with greater control and obtaining orders at short notice when they run out of stock. Breeding cockroaches often provides you with bargaining power when dealing with pet stores. Many store operators are more than happy to exchange cockroaches for other items such as reptiles, fish or pet supplies.

Most commercial and private customers like to give their animals a diversity of live foods and prefer to have both cockroaches and crickets. Meal worms are sometimes given as a treat, however cockroaches and crickets are the preferred choice from a nutritional perspective over the long term. Producing both live foods will provide your customers with better options and increase your customer base. Both species have different advantages and disadvantages as outlined in Table 1.

Table 1- Advantages and Disadvantages between Breeding Cockroaches and Crickets

Live food type	Advantages	Disadvantages
Cockroaches	<ul><li>Are more robust than crickets and if neglected they are more likely to survive.</li><li>Less maintenance requirements for commercial production (i.e. no breeding trays required).</li><li>Can be fed with a wider range of foods and of a lower quality than crickets (can tolerate fermenting and soggy foods).</li><li>Are long lived, living for many months or years depending on the species.</li><li>Very productive</li><li>Liked by most insectivorous animals.</li><li>Are social, able to be housed in high densities without significant cannibalism.</li></ul>	<ul><li>Cockroaches quickly scuttle under cover and out of reach from your animal.</li><li>Cockroaches are able to scale many smooth surfaces and are more difficult to contain and manage.</li><li>If not contained they can establish themselves in a house.</li><li>Some people have a "yuck" factor associated with keeping cockroaches.</li><li>A breeding colony can take 6 months or more to establish.</li></ul>
Crickets	<ul><li>Due to their jumping habit, crickets are often more effective at stimulating natural hunting behaviour than cockroaches or mealworms.</li><li>Some animals are fussy eaters and will only eat crickets, while refusing other live foods.</li><li>Crickets will generally be more active and more around the container, making them more available to be taken by animals.</li><li>Generally don't have the "yuck" factor associated with cockroaches</li><li>Have a quick start up time, only requiring 6 to have an established colony.</li></ul>	<ul><li>For commercial production require additional maintenance (spraying and set up of breeding trays).</li><li>Our "Zega Substrate Breeding System" has a similar maintenance requirement to cockroaches. The only additional job to be done is spraying the substrate every couple of weeks (see our website, www.zegaenterprises.com.au).</li><li>Are not as robust as cockroaches and generally require better and more consistent management.</li></ul>

<ul><li>Unable to climb many smooth surfaces (unlike cockroaches) and are consequently easier to manage and contain. This results in fewer escapees.</li><li>Prolific breeders that have a quick breeding lifecycle and fast production rate. A breeding colony can generally be set up within 6 weeks.</li></ul>	<ul><li>Have a relatively slow start up time, requiring around 6 months or more to establish a productive colony.</li><li>Have a relatively short shelf life, living for around 2-3 months.</li><li>Require higher quality wet foods (no fermenting or soggy foods)</li><li>Can be difficult to separate (grade) old large crickets which are close to dying and younger adult crickets which can be used for sale (when using a breeding method which has mixed aged groups in a single container)</li><li>Are not social, and will cannibalise if housed in high densities where proper management strategies are not in place.</li></ul>

Most people have given up on breeding crickets as conventional techniques are too much hassle and effort. This would traditionally involve daily spraying, cleaning, shaking poo from cartons, moving crickets from one container to another, diseases and smells. This is why most people have traditionally resorted to breeding cockroaches, which have lower maintenance requirements and greater breeding consistency. Thankfully our cricket breeding systems are very different. After 10 years of commercial production and experimentation, we have developed revolutionary new techniques that have halved maintenance, eliminated offensive odour and doubled production.

For example, using our unique "Zega Substrate System" (small scale production system) the "scrap vegies" from an average family can produce enough crickets to make" 4 pet store bought containers" each week…that's enough crickets to feed 4-12 bearded dragons (depending on feeding regime). For further information on how to breed a productive and low maintenance cricket colony, see our website (www.zegaenterprises.com.au) which outlines the benefits of "The Complete Cricket Breeding Manual".

1.2 How to Use This Manual

It is said that "A Picture Paints a Thousand Words". Throughout the manual we have provided more than, 145 photos, tables and diagrams to help you visualise the process. The sections that relate to "how to build" have been placed into tables and provide both written instructions and photos. This manual has been developed for both private and commercial production, and includes both "Basic" and "Advanced techniques".

Basic Method

These conventional methods are not necessarily the most efficient or durable options, however they are easier to construct and may be a good starting point for people who only want a basic and quick setup. This is a good starting point for beginners, who can then move to the efficient method at a later time.

Efficient Method- Overview

People who wish to have more advanced techniques which are more durable and productive with lower maintenance, should refer to the "Efficient Method" sections. These sections are essential for commercial production. They may involve a little extra effort upfront, however this will pay for itself many times over.

The "Efficient Method- Overview" provides an overview of the process. Tables relating to these sections have an orange background colour for quick reference.

Efficient Method- Detailed instructions

These sections provide detailed instructions for the "Efficient Method". They are very descriptive and provide a tried and tested formula to save you time with unnecessary experimentation. Tables which relate to these sections have an orange background colour for quick reference.

1.3 Conversions

Table 2- Conversion between Imperial and Metric Units

Conversion	Imperial/USA unit	Metric (SI) unit	Metric (SI) unit	Imperial/USA unit
Temperature	°C=degrees Celsius °F=Degrees Fahrenheit • °C = (°F − 32) ÷ 1.8 For example: (86°F-32) ÷ 1.8 = (36) ÷ 1.8 = 30°C • °F = (°C x 1.8) + 32 For example: (30°C x 1.8) + 32 = (54) + 32 = 86°F	10°C		50°F
		15°C		59°F
		20°C		68°F
		25°C		77°F
		30°C		86°F
		33°C		91.4°F
		40°C		104°F
Length	Inch	2.54 centimeters	Centimeter	0.39 inches
	Foot	30.48 centimeters	Meter	3.28 feet
	Yard	0.91 meters	Meter	1.09 yards
Volume	Teaspoon (UK)	5.92 milliliters	Milliliter	0.17 teaspoons (UK)
	Teaspoon (US)	4.93 milliliters		0.20 teaspoons (US)
	Tablespoon (UK)	17.76 milliliters	10 Milliliter	0.56 tablespoons (UK)
	Tablespoon (US)	14.79 milliliters		0.68 tablespoons (US)
	Fluid ounce (UK)	27.41 milliliters	100 milliliter	3.52 fluid ounces (UK)
	Fluid ounce (US)	28.57 milliliters		3.38 fluid ounces (US)
	Pint (UK)	0.57 liters	Liter	1.76 pints (UK)
	Pint (US)	0.47 liters		2.11 pints (US)
	Quart (UK)	1.14 liters		0.88 quarts (UK)
	Quart (US)	0.95 liters		1.06 quarts (US)
	Gallon (UK)	4.55 liters		0.22 gallon (UK)
	Gallon (US)	3.79 liters		0.26 gallons (US)
Weight	Ounce (weight)	27.35 grams	Gram	0.035 ounces
	Pound	0.45 kilograms	Kilogram	2.21 pounds
Power	1 kilowatt (KW)= 1000 watts			

The Complete Cockroach Breeding Manual

2.0 COCKROACH BIOLOGY

2.1 Anatomy

As shown in diagram 2.1 and 2.2 below, a cockroach's body is composed of three major body sections: head (front end), thorax (middle) and abdomen (back).

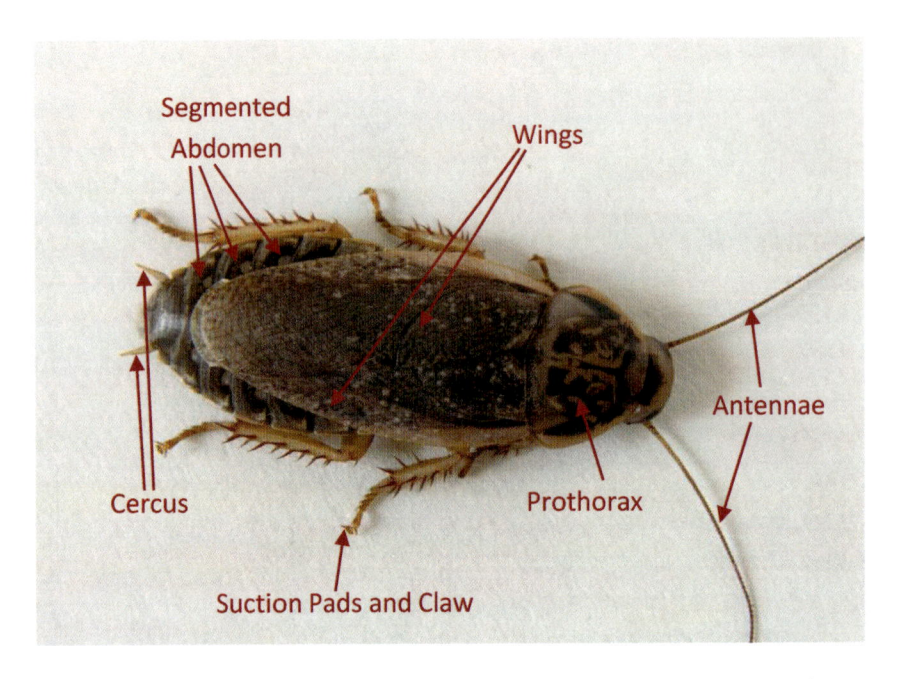

Diagram 2.1, Anatomy of a Cockroach (Nauphoeta cinerea)- Top view

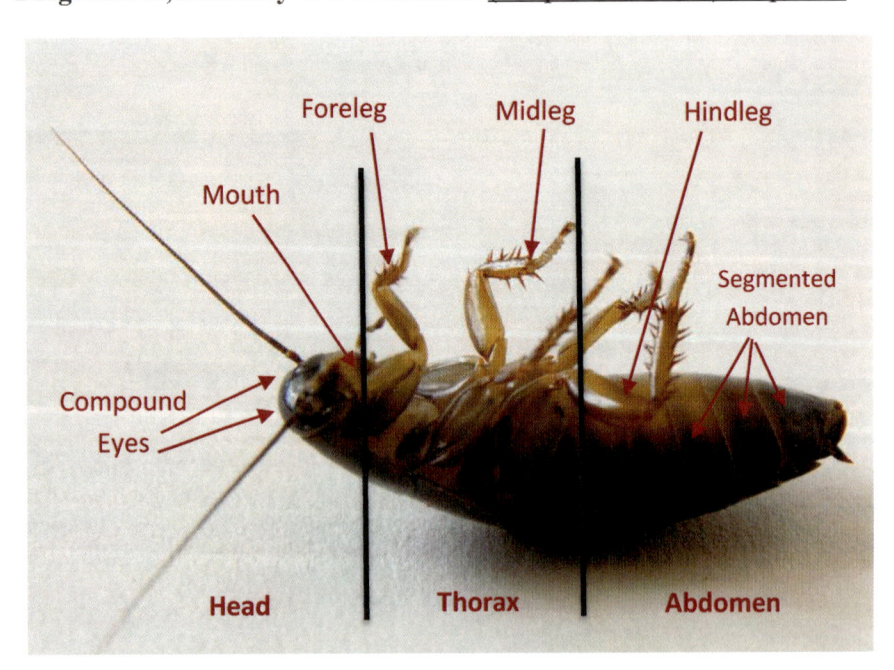

Diagram 2.2, Anatomy of a Cockroach (Nauphoeta cinerea)- Bottom view

A cockroach has the following anatomical features:

Eyes: Comprise of a thousand or more individual lenses, which allows them to see predators from multiple directions.

Sensory organs: Cerci are the two appendages found at the back of the animals, which can sense the smallest air changes. The legs of the cockroach are also sensitive to vibrations and touch which helps them avoid predators. The antennae (feelers) of the cockroach is used to smell.

Mouth: The mouth moves from side to side and can collect smell and taste.

Digestion: Salivary glands produce saliva which starts to break down food, which is the first stage of digestion. Cockroaches have a crop that stores food temporarily, before going into the stomach. Enzymes in the stomach break down food.

Fat stores: Fat bodies are located throughout the body, which store energy to be used as required.

Breathing: Insects due to their small size do not require a heart to circulate oxygen. Instead they have a series of internal tubes which diffuse oxygen throughout the body. The opening of these tubes are called spiracles and are generally located on the side of the cockroach's body.

Exoskeleton: is the outside hard covering which protects the cockroach. Insects don't have an internal skeleton like mammals, instead their body is supported by the outside (exo) skeleton. It comprises of segments which allows movement of the body.

Wings: Many species of cockroaches they have well developed wings which enables them to fly with positive lift. In other species (often ground or burrowing species) their wings are less well developed and they may not be able to fly, or can only fly downwards (a form of gliding).

Legs: All six legs are located on the thorax (middle section). At the end of the feet are very small suction pads and claws which can penetrate or stick onto many surfaces. This enables cockroaches the ability to climb many plastics and glass surfaces with ease.

2.2 Biology and Behaviour

Cockroaches are a diverse group of insects which are found in a wide range of habitats and have diverse behaviours. Taxonomically (classification), they belong to the Kingdom Animalia (animals), Phylum Arthropoda (segmented invertebrate), Class Insecta (insects), and Order Blattodea (cockroaches). Each species has its unique biology and behaviour, some of which described in Section 2.3 (Species Selection) for the more common species. Some of the more common features shared by most cockroaches is described below:

- **Food-** Are omnivorous eating a wide range of foods including animal and plant food sources. Food items include, fruit, meat, human left overs and leaves. In captivity, providing a combination of dry foods (i.e. cat/dog/chicken layer pellets) and wet foods (carrots, potato, apple, sweat potato, cabbage leaves etc.) is the best combination. This is covered in more detail in Section 5.0 (Food and Water Requirements).

- **Water-** Cockroaches will not survive long without water, but can survive approximately 3-4 weeks if given water and dry food. Providing water from a dispenser and through wet foods is best, however they can survive fine if provided with wet food daily.
- **Housing-** When given the choice, cockroaches will inhabit moist, warm, dark habitats close to food and water.
- **Breeding-** Most roaches are oviparous, with the eggs being located outside of the mother's body. This commonly referred to as "live bearing". The eggs are carried in an egg sac (ootheca), which are attached to her abdomen. Often the eggs are hidden or dropped just before they hatch. Other species carry their eggs after they are born. Some species continue to carry the hatching eggs and care for their young after they are born. It is important that this egg sac remain moist otherwise the eggs will not develop properly. Some species are ovoviviparous, with the ootheca located inside the mother's body.
- **Young-** Newly hatched roaches, are known as nymphs. When born their exoskeleton has not hardened and is white in color. At this stage they are prone to dehydration. Shortly after birth the exoskeleton hardens and they resemble small, wingless adult roaches.
- **Molting-** Nymphs undergo a number of molts before becoming adults. The period between each molt is known as an instar. Each instar results in the cockroach becoming more adult like.
- **Lifespan-** Some species live for a few months, others live for more than 2 years.
- **Predators-** In the wild cockroaches are predated on by a wide range of insectivorous animals such as reptiles, mammals, birds and predatory insects (wasps, prey mantis). The spores of Entomopathogenic fungi attach to cockroaches slowly consuming their insect prey. This is thought to be why cockroaches clean themselves regularly.
- **Behavior-** Most species can flatten themselves in order to bit in tight crevices or through floor boards. Cockroaches by nature do not like to be out in the open and will scuttle towards cover when exposed.
- **Communication-** Cockroaches produce pheromones (chemicals) as a form of communication. These chemicals attract other cockroaches, with many species cohabiting the same area.
- **Substrate-** Many species enjoy living in substrate (soil, leaves), however it is not recommended to add this in captivity, as it is hard to clean, quickly becomes unhygienic and makes collecting animals for harvest difficult.
- **Temperature-** Most species kept in captivity are from tropical areas, requiring a minimum temperature of 20-25 degrees. Productive breeding will require higher temperatures between 30-35 degrees Celsius. Refer to Table 17 (Chapter 7.0- Heating and Storage) for further details. Low temperatures is one of the main reason, a colonies productivity drops off, or you get deaths.
- **Humidity-** Most species require medium to high humidity ranges which can be obtained from a water source (i.e. water dispenser) or wet foods. Humidity is important to prevent dehydration and to facilitate molting. Once a cockroach has lost its old protective exoskeleton, it is prone to dehydration. Where cockroaches are dying during their molt, humidity should be increased. Too much humidity can create harmful pathogens such as fungi, bacteria and mites.

- **Harvesting-** A cockroach colony can take 6 months or longer to become fully established, with a full range of animals. Avoid taking a large number of animals until the colony is operating optimally.
- **Containing cockroaches-** Some species of cockroaches are very efficient at climbing most plastic and glass surfaces. Barrier creams can be smeared to the top inner surface of a container (5cm wide) to prevent them from escaping. Vaseline and olive oil can be used, however they become messy collecting detritus etc. An alternative product is painting Fluon which is difficult for cockroaches to climb.

2.3 Species Selection

A number of different species of cockroach are bred around the world for private and commercial production. Due to the wide range of species bred in captivity, we have provided a brief description of the common species, with links to websites for further information.

Once or twice a year you will want to add additional stock to your collection, to prevent inbreeding. Ideally you will choose a species which can be easily accessed by local pet stores or commercial breeders.

In Australia the speckled cockroach (Nauphoeta cinerea) is a common species bred for live food, and our experience relates to this species. Most of the husbandry and general breeding requirements for cockroaches is common across most species, however check the below websites for your selected species, to ensure their specific needs are met. Below is a summary of the characteristics of some of the most common species:

Dubia Cockroach (Blaptica dubia)

- An easy and reliable species to breed, and are consequently very popular[1].
- A relatively small cockroach that is suitable to feeding smaller animals[1].
- Slow moving species, which are less shy than other species[1]
- Live bearing species[1]
- Are poor climbers, and are not good at scaling smooth surfaces[1]
- Species is sexually dimorphic, with males having larger wings than the females[1]
- Males have shorter lifespans than females[1].
- Require mid humidity levels, however are more tolerable to low humidity most species. They do much better when good moisture is provided[1].

Websites with further information:

- http://www.nyworms.com/dubiacare.htm (information provided above[1])
- http://.ntlworld.com/bandung/roaches/

Madagascar Hissing Cockroach (Gromphradorhina portentosa)

- Are a large species that are well suited as feeders for all the larger species of lizards[1].
- Are live bearers, with a gestation period of about 60 days. The nymphs are born about 6mm (1/4 inch) in size with approximately 30 born at one time[1].
- Adults are not aggressive to young. With higher temperatures, the nymphs can reach adult size in about 3 months. With less heat it may take five months or longer[1].
- This species can live and breed 2 to 3 years or longer. Approximately two or three batches of young can be produced each year[1].
- They are good climbers and a barrier cream (Vaseline, Fluon) is required to prevent escapees.
- Require low to medium humidity.

Websites with further information:

- http://www.nyworms.com/dubiacare.htm (information provided above[1])
- http://.ntlworld.com/bandung/roaches/
- http://users.usachoice.net/~swb/pet_arthropod/hiss.htm

Discoid Cockroaches (Blaberus discoidales)

- Popular mid-sized cockroach[1].
- Non-climbing, non-flying species that produce live young[1].
- Tropical species, native to northern parts of South America.
- Shy species[1].
- Substrate is not required, however they enjoy burrowing if substrate if provided[1].
- This species require a good supply of moisture at all times[1].
- Require low to medium humidity.
- Slow to breed, but productive when there is sufficient breeding adults[1]

Websites with further information:

- http://www.nyworms.com/dubiacare.htm (information provided above[1])
- http://.ntlworld.com/bandung/roaches/

Orange Headed Cockroaches (Eublaberus prosticus)

- Have a bright orange head when they reach adult hood[1].
- Good productive breeders[1].
- Non climbing, non-flying species[1]
- Live bearing[1]
- Nymphs are a deep red color[1].
- Produce a defensive odor when disturbed.
- Tropical species, requiring high temperatures[1].

2.0- Cockroach Biology

Websites with further information:

- http://www.nyworms.com/dubiacare.htm (information provided above[1])

Speckled or Lobster Cockroaches (Nauphoeta cinerea)

- Life span approximately 12 months[2].
- Worldwide distribution, original home believed to be East Africa[2].
- Have approximately 26-40 eggs at a time[2].
- Are exceptionally good climbers, being able to scale most surfaces, and often escape without proper barrier creams such as Vaseline or Fluon[2].
- I have found that escapees of this species can establish in houses and sheds. Photo of this species is shown in photo 2.3 below.

Websites with further information:

- http://www.herpshop.com.au/CareSheets/FeaderRoach.html (information provided above[2])

2.3

3.0 CONTAINER DESIGN AND CONSTRUCTION

For small scale production many people may wish to use existing household containers such as fish tanks, plastic tubs or unused storage containers. If you wish to produce more efficiently (or on a larger scale) you will need to construct purpose built containers. The main design considerations for a container are outlined below (instructions how to build container components are outlined in following sections):

3.1 Choosing a Container

The most important factor in choosing a container is height. I typically use containers that have a 70L capacity, 65cm long, 42cm wide and 40cm high. A large container with high sides has the following advantages:

3.1

- Allows sufficient height to place large egg cartons and corrugated apple cartons (stop apples from bruising during transport, found at your local supermarket), to be placed vertically in the container. The apple cartons are folded in half and can be placed inside the container without needing to be cut. Alternatively the large square egg cartons (25cm by 25cm) from fast food restaurants, bakeries (try your local supermarket) or egg producers, can be placed inside without cutting. This saves a lot of time when you have to replace the cartons from numerous containers. Photo 3.1 shows an apple cardboard carton before and after being folded, and a large egg carton from a fast food restaurant.
- Having adequate container height, length and volume allows you to accommodate sufficient cardboard cartons which will comfortably accommodate 500-700+ large cockroaches (with 70L container described above) with minimal cannibalism. Two of these containers at harvest will typically produce approximately 1200 cockroaches which is a common quantity purchased by commercial clients (Refer to Section 9.4- Economics for further details).
- Try to retain approximately 10-15cm between the top of the cartons and the lid, and choose a smooth surface plastic. This will allow you to apply a barrier cream which prevents cockroaches from climbing out (Refer to Section 3.6- Barrier Cream).
- The containers are not too heavy or bulky, and can therefore be easily moved and cleaned as required
- Opaque containers are preferential to clear plastic as the animals feel more secure and prefer to lay eggs in darkness (predominantly nocturnal in the wild).

The Complete Cockroach Breeding Manual

Tip: Containers with a good quality plastic are more durable and are less likely to crack whilst handling and drilling/cutting during construction. You get what you pay for, so a good quality container may be more expensive initially, but will last for many years. If you are uncertain of the quality of the container, purchase one initially and trial it before purchasing more.

Some containers have irregular shaped ends so they slide into each other. This limits the amount of flat surface you can cut a ventilation port in. Preferentially try to choose a container with flat plastic on all sides.

3.2 Lids

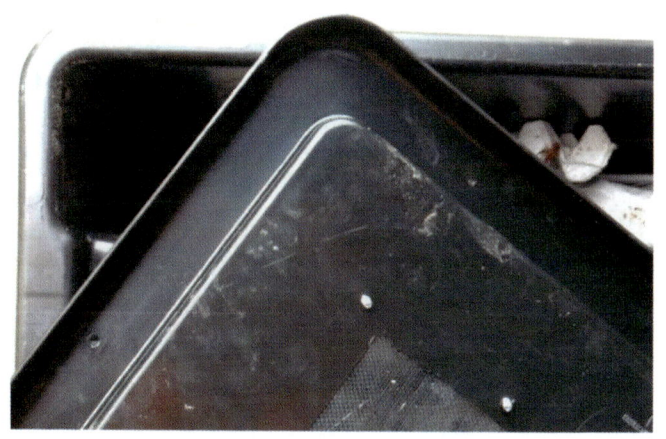

Choosing an effective lid type will prevent pest species from entering (foreign cockroaches, spiders, geckoes) and prevent cockroaches from escaping.

Many lid systems are effective, including the one shown in photo 3.2. This consists of a flattened edge (U shaped) lid which is commonly used in restaurant food containers to prevent the entry of cockroaches and other food pests.

This lid type is also effective for breeding crickets if you wish to breed both species.

3.2

3.3 Ventilation

Cockroaches require good ventilation, otherwise they overheat and die in hot weather. A well designed container will allow fan forced or ambient air to ventilate the whole space. This is achieved by installing ventilation ports at both ends of the container and in the lid. (Refer to photo 3.6, 3.8 and figure 3.3). In figure 3.3, end "A" is the front of the shelving (where a fan can be placed. End" B" is the rear of the shelving (against wall); the pink rectangle area (hatched) represents the food tray and black solid line at both ends are air vents. Wavy lines are cartons. This setup has the following advantages:

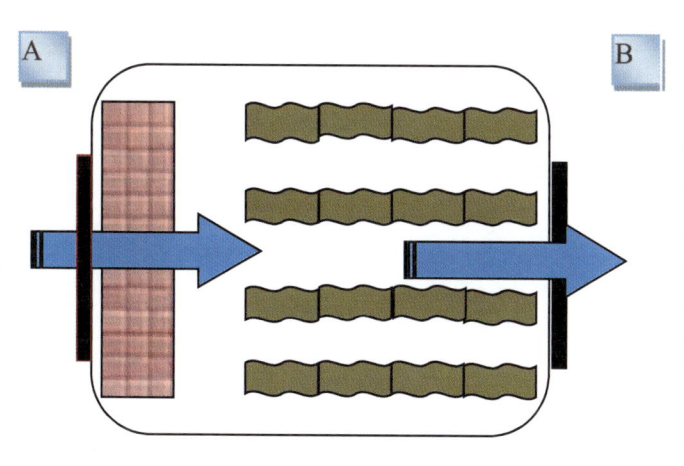

Figure 3.3- Air Flow through a Container

The Complete Cockroach Breeding Manual

3.0- Container Design and Construction

- A fan can be placed at the front to blow cool air through the container (at end "A"). As the cardboard cartons are orientated in the same direction (length ways) the cool air is able to move from one end, through the cardboard cartons and out the other end. Had the vents or the cardboard cartons been placed the other direction it would block the cool air from passing through the container.
- The air circulation not only provides cool air but helps remove odour and gas build up in hot weather.
- This orientation also ensures that the cockroaches in each cardboard carton have access to fresh air and food/water at the end of each carton (Refer to next section). If cartons were placed in the other direction they would have to move to the end of the carton then walk to the food.
- As all cartons give good access to food and water, cockroaches are more likely to spread out across the full length of the container and not congregate near the food source. This spreads the cockroaches over a wider area and reduces overcrowding.

A large ventilation vent is placed in the lid as hot air rises and this removes excess heat. In cooler times of the year, heat can be retained by placing a breathable material (towel, sheet) over the top of the lid. Due to the ventilation in the lid, it is not recommended to stack containers directly on top of each other.

3.4 Feeding Port

3.4

A feeding port allows you to place wet food into the feeding tray without the need to pull the container out, and open the lid. This is useful in intensive situations where containers are tightly packed above each other and the shelving is not high enough to open from the top. If however you have sufficient room above to open the lid, the feeding port is not required.

The feeder port is made from a water tank inlet pipe (threaded pipe) and removable filter (metal screen that prevents mosquitos getting into water tank) as shown in photo 3.4. The removable filter is not threaded and can be pushed into and out of the threaded pipe (Refer to photo 3.5). A feeding port allows you to restock the food to numerous containers in only a few minutes, using a narrow measuring jug (Refer to photo 5.2).

The Complete Cockroach Breeding Manual

3.5 Screening

Special consideration is needed to be given to the type of mesh used to cover ventilation holes. Normal fibreglass fly screen is not suitable as some species of cockroaches eat it, resulting in escapees.

Aluminium screening cannot be eaten, is robust and self-supporting. Photo 3.5 shows how this screening attached to a container.

3.5

3.6 Barrier Cream

Many species of cockroach are very good climbers as a result of adhesive pads and claws on the end of their feet. This enables them to feed and penetrate small cracks or stick to surfaces.

Barrier creams are applied to the top 5cm of a container to prevent cockroaches from climbing out. Vaseline, olive oil or "Fluon Insect film" (can be purchased online) can be used for this purpose. Fluon is applied as a white paint, but dries and eventually becomes a powder. This can be rubbed off, so care must be taken to avoid disturbing this area. Under normal circumstances, Fluon would need to be applied every couple of months or as required.

3.7 Component Set-up

Photo 5.3 shows how the various components are placed within a container:

<u>Egg and Apple Cartons</u>

Are placed in a vertical position so that droppings fall to the floor of the container. This will improve hygiene, and reduces maintenance (cartons placed horizontally need to be shaken and cleaned daily).

Tip: Talk with your local fast food restaurant (e.g. McDonalds) or supermarket manager and organise to have them stockpiled for you. Note that most managers will want you to pick them up on a regular basis as piles of cartons are a potential trip hazard, fire risk, harbour vermin or breach health regulations. Mondays and weekends are usually their busiest days and your best periods for obtaining the most cartons.

Try to collect them in quiet periods so that the counter staff aren't put out by having to collect your cartons in their busiest periods. As many restaurants /supermarkets have a number of new staff changing shifts regularly, be prepared that some people will forget to collect cartons. To minimise this, collect the cartons at the same time and days of the week, so that you speak with the same staff familiar with the routine. Most importantly make sure you collect the cartons on the agreed pick up day/time.

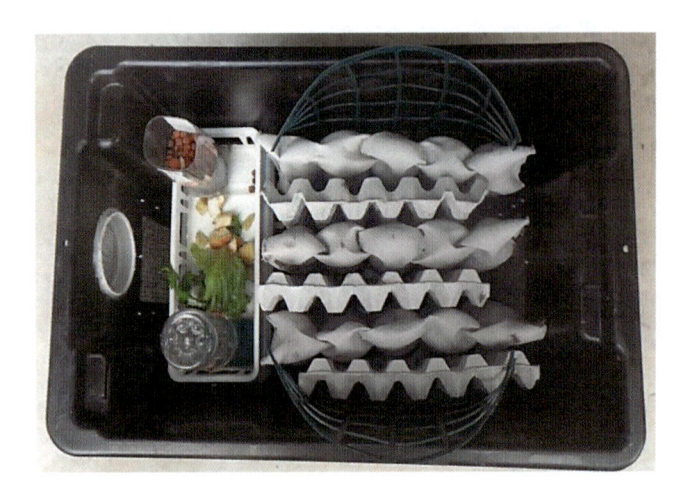

Automated Food and Water Dispensers

Are placed at the same end as the feeding port. A rectangular food tray holds both the food and water dispenser with wet food in the middle. The food tray allows for all components to be removed quickly and acts as a storage area for wet foods dispensed through the feeding port.

Trellis Basket

3.6

Plastic garden trellis is bent into a "U" shape and wrapped around so that all the cartons can be removed quickly for easy cleaning (Refer to photo 3.6). Avoid wrapping the mesh over the top of the cartons (i.e. "O" shape) as this will squeeze the cartons together at the top and bend them out of shape over time.

3.8 Making a Container

Basic Method

Building a container can be as simple or as complicated as your needs require. Some ideas are outlined below:

- Make an aluminium screen frame and placing this over the top of a container such as a fish tank, plastic container or tub.
- Cutting holes into the ends and lid of a container, and attaching screening with duct tape, glue gun or rivets.
- Where pests aren't an issue (usually closed rooms with screening), some people don't use lids.

3.0- Container Design and Construction

Efficient Method- Overview

A summary of this design is outlined in Table 3 and a completed unit is shown in photo 3.7a. Note the ventilation ports within the lid and container ends, and a feeding port at one end.

3.7a

Table 3- Overview of Constructing a Container- Efficient Method

Construction Method	Photo
1) CUTTING VENTILATION AND FEEDING PORTS • Mark the outline of the ventilation ports at each end of the container and the lid • Mark the outline of the feeding port at one end. • Using tin snips or jig saw, cut ventilation ports at the ends and into the lid of the container (Refer to photo 3.7b). Leave sufficient room on the edges to attach rivets into the screen.	3.7b
• **INSTALLING SCREENING TO CONTAINER** Cut aluminium screening slightly wider than the ventilation ports so they can be attached using rivets. • Attach aluminium screening with rivets and silicon adhesive (Refer to photo 3.8). Another method is using a soldering iron and press screening into the plastic.	3.8

The Complete Cockroach Breeding Manual

3.0- Container Design and Construction

- Place a bead of flexible silicon adhesive around the edges to prevent small cockroaches from squeezing between the screens. Push the adhesive through the screening with a spatula (i.e. ice cream stick) so it bonds with the plastic (Refer to photo 3.8).
-

2) INSTALLING SCREENING TO LID

- Same steps as outlined in instruction 2 above.
- Silicon can be spread along the edges using a spatula (Refer to photo 3.9).

3.9

3) INSTALLING FEEDING PORT (OPTIONAL- REFER TO SECTION 3.4)

- Cut the irrigation end piping flush with the inside of the container
- Push pipe through hole and mark a cut off line on the inside of box.
- Attach with silicon adhesive (Refer to photo 3.10 and 3.11).

Tip: Silicon adhesive is flexible and best used for screening, fixed structures such as pipe are best secured with constructive adhesive which is not flexible

3.10

3.11

The Complete Cockroach Breeding Manual

3.0- Container Design and Construction

Efficient Method- Detailed

Table 4- Detailed Instructions for Constructing a Container-Efficient Method

Construction Method	Photo
1) CUTTING VENTILATION AND FEEDING PORTS a) Start with drawing rectangular ventilation ports at the ends of the container and lid using a ruler and marker pen. Below are some basic concepts to follow: • Retain at least a 3cm gap around all ventilation ports to provide sufficient space to attach screen mesh with rivets. (Refer to photo 3.12- distance indicated by arrow A). Another method is using a soldering iron, press the screening into the plastic. • Feeding port should be placed as high as possible to maximise the amount of area available for the ventilation port below. The location of the feeder hole can be traced using the irrigation piping as a template. • Avoid removing more than 60% of the surface area of the container end, to retain sufficient heat. • Retain at least 4cm of plastic between the bottom of the container and ventilation port to prevent detritus coming out during cleaning activities (i.e. when tilting the detritus to one end and removing). (Refer to photo 3.12- arrow B indicates width of plastic to be retained). • The lids of some containers buckle and have trouble closing if you don't retain sufficient plastic on the edge of the lid and the ventilation port. This problem is overcome with most containers, by retaining a minimum width of 5-7cm around the edge (Refer to photo 3.13- arrows indicate width of plastic to be retained). b) Once the template has been drawn, cut the hole out using a jigsaw or hand metal cutters. This job is made easier if a pilot hole is drilled first at each corner, to provide access for the electric jig saw or snippers (Refer to photos 3.12 and 3.13).	3.12 3.13
2) INSTALLING SCREENING TO CONTAINER c) Collect the plastic off cuts from the ventilation ports, and use them as a template to outline the edge of the aluminium mesh (Refer to photo 3.14 - "top section" plastic off cuts, "middle" aluminium screening. Cut the mesh an additional 2.5 cm wider than the plastic templates to allow the mesh edges to be riveted to the container.	

The Complete Cockroach Breeding Manual

3.0- Container Design and Construction

d) Place the aluminium screening over the ventilation vents and drill a hole through the screening into the container along the edges.

3.14

e) Use a rivet gun to attach aluminium screening to the container (Refer to photo 3.15). The spacing between each rivet must allow enough tension to prevent cockroaches from escaping. A distance of approximately 7-10cm is usually sufficient. Other attachment methods include hot glue gun, clear constructive adhesive or duct tape. Rivets are more durable however, and handle the twisting and bending that occurs during cleaning. Long open aluminium rivets (rust proof) with a diameter of 3.2 mm (1/8") and a grip depth of 7.9 mm (5/16") should provide enough depth to penetrate thick plastics commonly used for containers.

3.15

Tip: Do not over tension the screening as you rivet, as this will cause the screen to buckle and twist- light tension is best.

f) Place a bead of flexible silicon adhesive around the edges to prevent small cockroaches from squeezing between the screens. Push the adhesive through the screening with a spatula (i.e. ice cream stick) so it bonds with the plastic (Refer to photo's 3.16 and 3.17).

3.16

3.17

The Complete Cockroach Breeding Manual

3.0- Container Design and Construction

3) INSTALLING SCREENING TO CONTAINER LID

g) Process for attaching screen to lid is same as attaching screen to container as outlined in instruction 2 above.

h) Photo 3.18 shows a bead of silicon being applied along the edges prior to flattening them with a spatula.

3.18

4) INSTALLING FEEDING PORT (OPTIONAL-REFER TO SECTION 3.4)

i) Photo 3.19 shows the "water tank overflow pipe" components - "left" screen plug, "right" threaded pipe.

j) The location of the feeding port is outlined in instruction 1, above- "Cutting ventilation and feeding ports".
Drill a pilot hole into the plastic and use a jig saw to make the circular cut. Do not cut too wide as you are aiming to have a tight fit. This is achieved by cutting the hole a fraction smaller than required and using a rough file to widen the hole manually.

k) Place the piping into the hole and mark a line with a marker on the inside of the piping where it becomes flush with the container wall. (Note blue line on piping in photo 3.20- Refer to arrow).

l) Remove the feeding port from the container and using a hacksaw cut excess piping so it fits flush with the inside of the container.

m) Use constructive adhesive (using a silicon gun) to attach the feeding port to the container. Scrape excess glue with disposable spatula (i.e. paddle pop stick).

3.19

3.20

The Complete Cockroach Breeding Manual

4.0 BREEDING
4.1 Breeding Overview

As outlined in earlier sections most cockroaches are oviparous, with the eggs being located outside of the mother's body. This commonly referred to as "live bearing". The eggs are carried in an egg sac (ootheca), which are attached to her abdomen. Often the eggs are hidden or dropped just before they hatch. Other species carry their eggs after they are born.

Some species continue to carry the hatching eggs and care for their young after they are born. It is important that this egg sac remain moist otherwise the eggs will not develop properly. If low humidity conditions persist for long periods the productivity of the colony will reduce or stop breeding. Some species are ovoviviparous, with the ootheca located inside the mother's body.

Newly hatched roaches, are known as nymphs. When born their exoskeleton has not hardened and is white in color. At this stage they are prone to dehydration. Shortly after birth the exoskeleton hardens and they resemble small, wingless adult roaches. Nymphs undergo a number of molts before becoming adults. The period between each molt is known as an instar. Each instar results in the cockroach becoming more adult like. Some species live for a few months, others live for more than 2 years.

Most species kept in captivity are from tropical areas, requiring a minimum temperature of 20-25 degrees Celsius (68- 77 degrees Fahrenheit). Productive breeding will require higher temperatures between 30-35 degrees Celsius (86-95 degrees Fahrenheit). Refer to table 12 (Chapter 7.1- Heating and Humidity Requirements) for further details. Low temperatures is one of the main reason, a colonies productivity drops off, or you get deaths.

Each species of cockroach has its own unique breeding strategy and lifecycle. Species specific information can be obtained from Section 2.3 (Species Selection).

4.2 Zega Cockroach Breeding System

This system can be used for small scale and large scale production. It comprises of the following components:

1) A "false floor" (wire rack raised by plastic supports) just above the bottom of the container so that the cartons and food are lifted off the floor. This prevents the cartons from making contact with detritus which falls to the bottom. This greatly increases the life of the cartons which can last around 6-9 months (normally would need to be replaced weekly).
2) Refer to Section 3.0 (Container Design and Construction) for general container design and component set up.
3) A trellis basket is used to hold together and move all the cartons together for cleaning (Refer to Section 3.7 for details).
4) A schematic diagram of the setup is shown in diagram 4.1 below. How to build instructions can be found in Table 7- How to Make a "Zega Cockroach Breeding System"

4.0- Breeding

Figure 4.1- Diagrammatic Representation of a "Zega Cockroach Breeding System"

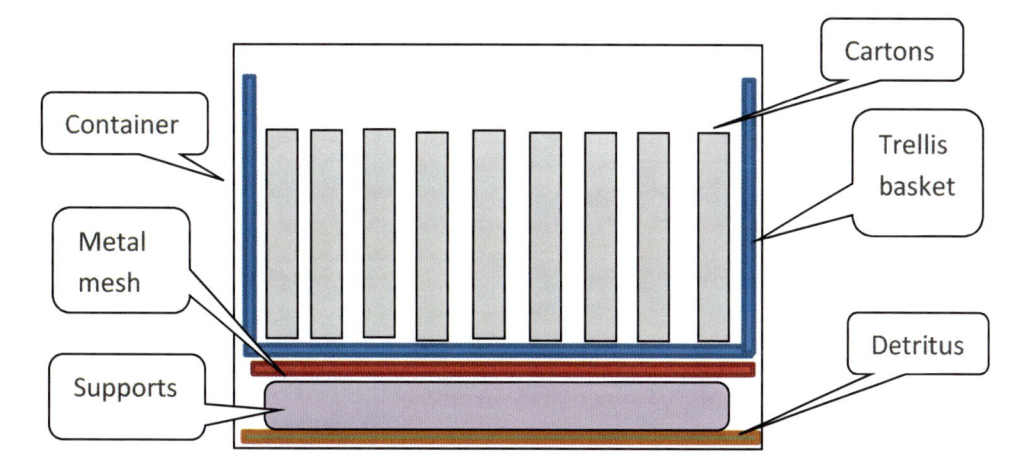

Labels: Container, Metal mesh, Supports, Cartons, Trellis basket, Detritus

Note: Food trays and food/water dispensers are located on top of metal mesh.

Materials

The following materials are required to make a "Zega Cockroach Breeding System":
- A standard container as described in Section 3.7.
- Plastic trellis used in gardens as a support for creeping plants (Refer to item A in photo 4.2)
- Metal mesh (aluminium or galvanised steel) or a large baking cooling rack- Refer to item B in photo 4.2.
- Two lengths of "L" shaped plastic roof flashing (Refer to photo 4.3). This can be found at the roofing section of your local hardware store.

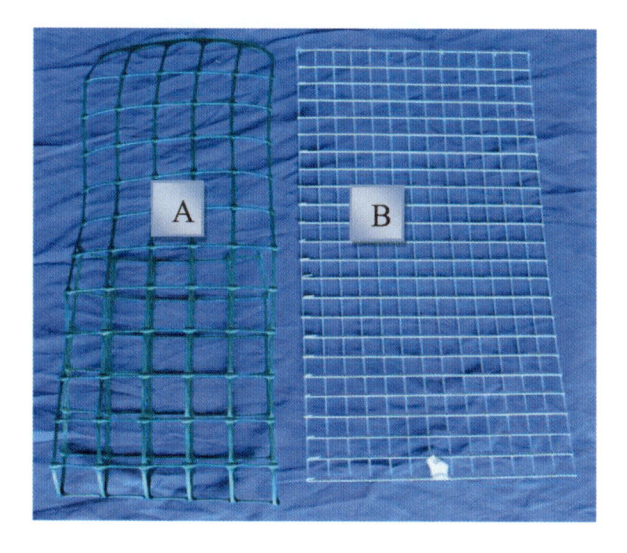

4.2

4.3

The Complete Cockroach Breeding Manual

4.0- Breeding

Table 5- How to Make a "Zega Cockroach Breeding System"

Component or Construction Method	Photo
1) **"BUILD THE CONTAINER"** • Refer to table 4- Detailed Instructions for Constructing a Container- Efficient Method and photo 4.4	4.4
1) **SPACERS** Purpose/overview: • These act as spacers to raise the metal mesh and cartons off the bottom of the container. (Refer to photo 4.5). How to build • Use a hacksaw to cut the plastic. • Cut two pieces of plastic "L" sections 2-3cm shorter than the width of the container bottom, so they fit without jamming.	4.5
2) **METAL MESH** Purpose/overview: • The metal mesh supports the cartons and food trays above. Detritus falls through the mesh to the bottom.	

The Complete Cockroach Breeding Manual

How to build

- Cut the metal mesh to the shape of the container base. This is made easier by turning over the container and using the base as a template by marking its outline on the mesh.
- Alternatively you can use a baking tray, with metal legs. If they have legs, you will not need to make the spacers described above.
- When cutting the mesh (bolt cutters, angle grinder or metal cutters), make it 2cm smaller on each side so that it fits in the container without jamming. Place the mesh over the "Spacers" as shown in photo 4.6.

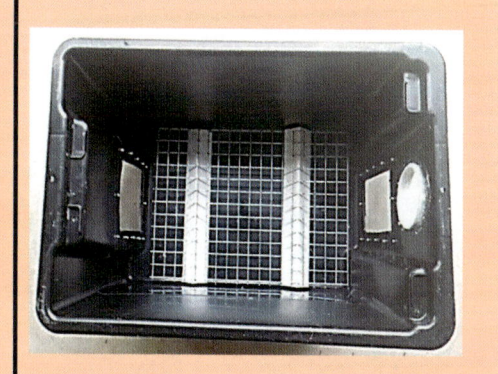

4.6

3) **TRELLIS BASKET**

Purpose/overview:

- The trellis basket is used to hold together and move all the cartons together for cleaning.
- This allows all the cartons to be transferred to a separate cleaning container, so you can clean the breeding container (Refer to Section 3.7- Component Set-up and 8.2- Cleaning).

How to build

- Get a length of trellis and bent into a "U" shape so it covers under the containers and up both sides of the container (Refer to photo 4.7).
- Measure this distance and then cut to size.

4.7

1) **FINAL SET UP**

- Place the "spacers" on the bottom of the container and then place metal mesh on top of these as shown in photo 4.6.
- Stack together a pile of cartons alternating egg and then apple cartons. The cartons are alternated as egg cartons placed next to each other will fold into each other.
- The apple cartons have the advantage of making a dark closed space which cockroaches like. The egg cartons

4.8

have the advantage of having a large surface area, providing a large area for cockroaches to make home.
- Place the trellis basket around the cartons and place on top of the wire mesh.
- Place food tray and water/food dispensers to the end with the food port. The final set up is shown in photo 4.8.
- Container is ready for cockroaches to be added. When buying cockroaches get a mix of all size groups, large, medium and small. Get as many as you can afford to fast track the colony. Consider buying large bulk packs of 1000, you may need to get a special order in from your pet store.

5.0 FOOD AND WATER REQUIREMENTS
5.1 Food and Water Components

Basic Method:

The most basic method for providing food and water is placing a food/water bowl to one end of the container. Another method is placing the food/water bowls in the middle with cartons on both sides. This makes access to food easier, but you have to cut more cartons.

Cockroaches will drown in water if something is not placed in the water. Some people place pebbles, cotton wool, sponge or hydration crystals (used to provide water for plants-found at nurseries) in the water to prevent cockroaches from drowning.

The disadvantage of these methods is that they often get dirty and unhygienic quickly, or need to be regularly topped up for a large active colony. An active colony in a 70L container described in Section 3.1 (Choosing a Container) will drink 500-700ml of water/week in hot weather.

Hydration crystals quickly dehydrate (shrink in size) and require regular top up otherwise they stick to the container making them hard to clean.

5.1   5.2

Efficient Method

To reduce ongoing maintenance and the overcome the issues described above the following automated feeding/watering dispensers have been developed to minimise feeding and cleaning. As shown in photo 5.1, the basic food tray comprises of a long narrow tray that holds both food and water dispensers at the ends and wet foods (fruits and vegetables) in the middle. The tray is cut in a way that creates holes that double as handles. The tray can then be removed by lifting from the middle. The advantage of a tray system (as opposed to individual food/water containers) is that all components can be removed together, reducing maintenance time, space and potential spills.

All dispenser trays (dry food and water) should be rectangular which take up less space than circular dishes, leaving more room for cartons to increase productivity. Automated dispensers allow food and water to be dispensed as required, with refilling occurring only 7-10 days as required. If you go away for extended periods (up to 10-18 days) the size of the reservoirs can be increased to cater for longer periods without the need for refilling. Wet foods can be placed into the container by either:

a) Opening the lid and placing the food directly into the tray or;
b) Placing the food through a feeding port and falling into food tray below (Refer to photo 5.2 and Section 3.4- Feeding Port).

The feeding port is only necessary if you stack your containers one above another and the shelving hasn't left enough space to open the lid as shown in photo 5.2. A narrow measuring jug (with handles cut off) can be used to measure standard food quantities and to place food through the port and into the tray.

5.2 Dry Food- Nutrition and Processing

Nutritional Requirements

The key requirements for cockroach growth are protein, calcium, and energy. Researchers studying locusts and other insects found that they would continue to eat relentlessly until their daily protein requirements have been met. Once a locust has eaten a set amount of protein, it stops eating even if other food is provided. The same concept works for humans and other animals. If you provide high quality food with high protein it is likely that the amount of food cockroaches eat will decrease saving you money. Having a sufficient calcium intake, is important for an animal which undergoes regular molts.

Food consumption by small cockroaches is relatively small, but will significantly increase when they reach medium size. Food consumption reaches its maximum at the young adult stage (active egg production) and then gradually decreases with age.

A wide range of pellet dry foods can be used to feed cockroaches. Some people use, cat/dog/chicken layer/guinea pig/rabbit pellets. This becomes confusing when you go to a pet store and are confronted with this wide range of food types and different brands. My preference is cat/dog food mixed with Chicken Layer pellets. The chicken layer pellets have high calcium as they are used by laying chickens for egg production. To help you understand which brands are the best option, Table 6 shows the relative nutritional information for a variety of dry foods.

- As cats are mostly carnivorous, their food has a higher protein percentage than either dog or chicken food. Kitten cat food is higher in crude fat and fibre than adult cat food. High protein is beneficial for cricket growth; however it is the more expensive option. Cat food is the preferred choice when choosing a dry food for gut loading.

- Dogs are more omnivorous (eat meats and plant material) and consequently the protein component is lower and consists of both animal and plant proteins. However they are usually cheaper than cat food. When purchasing dog food look for "working dog" and "puppy dog" food which would typically have higher protein and fat content due to their higher energy and nutritional requirements.

Table 6- Nutritional Comparison between Different Dry Food Types

Nutrient category	Chicken – Pullet starter (hatchlings up to 8 weeks)[1] (%) © Ridley AgriProducts 2007	Chicken- Top layer (adult laying chickens) (%) © Ridley AgriProducts 2007	Cat food- Kitten (%) © Purina International	Cat food- Adult (%) © Purina International	Dog food – Puppy (%) © Purina International	Dog food – Adult (%) © Purina International
Protein	18.5	15.5	**40**	**40**	28	26
Crude fat	2.5	2.5	**18**	16	**18**	16
Crude fibre	6	**6**	3.5	2	3	3
Calcium	1	**3.6**	1	0.85	1	1

Note: items in bold indicate highest levels for each nutrient category (read horizontally)
[1] "Hatchling starter" for hatchlings from birth to 8 weeks

- Chicken food used for hatchlings (chicken pullet starter) is generally high in protein (for fast muscle growth) but low in calcium (too young to lay eggs). Chicken pellets used by laying chickens (top layer pellets) are high in calcium (for laying eggs) and slightly lower in protein as they are no longer growing. When choosing chicken food I prefer to use layer pellets as the main source of calcium for a dry food mix.

- Where possible pick cat/dog foods with high calcium levels, although this is not essential if mixing foods with layer pellets. If you choose a low calcium brand you can add powdered milk (refer to dry food recipe below). If possibly try to choose a small sized pellet (i.e. puppy or kitten food), as this won't need to be ground down much.

5.0- Food and Water Requirements

- I have found that a good compromise between cost and quality is achieved using a high quality dog food mixed with chicken layer pellets. In this way you get both high protein and fats (dog food) and high calcium (chicken layer pellets).

- Other dry food options to consider is rat/mice, rabbit/guinea pig pellets.

Dry Food Recipe

Below is a standard food recipe for cockroaches:

- 1 part (by volume or weight) high protein dog food
- 1 part (by volume or weight) high calcium layer chook pellets
- 1 part (by volume or weight) high protein cat food (optional, for normal food requirements but recommended for gut loading)
- 0.5 part (by volume or weight) fish pellets/flakes. (Optional for normal food requirements, but recommend for gut loading)

5.3

Processing

A full range of food sizes is required to cater for cockroaches of various sizes. As shown in photo 5.3, aim to achieve an equal mix of small particles (up to 1mm), medium particles (1-2mm) and larger particles (2-5mm).

If you find that the blender is making too much powder and not breaking up the larger pellets adequately, you can sift the mixture separating large and small particles. The larger semi-broken pellets can then be put back into the blender and further processed to the correct size.

Storage

To save on costs it is recommended to buy dry foods in bulk. The correct storage method is essential to prevent them from being infested with fungi, weevils or other insects. Below are some general principles to consider when storing and purchasing large quantities of food:

- Try not to purchase more food than you can use in 4-6 months. Storage methods generally do not allow for food to be stored in a fresh, nutritional manner greater than this time. This is particularly important in tropical environments.

- Place the contents of opened bags into air tight containers which will prevent moisture and humidity entering and reduce fungal infections.

5.0- Food and Water Requirements

- As shown in photo 5.4, bulk quantities of raw ingredients can be stored in 20L bucket containers found at your local hardware store (Refer to photo 5.4) Choose containers that are air and water tight (i.e. used to store paints/plasterboard paste and other products that need to retain moisture).

- As shown in photo 5.5 medium quantities of ground ingredients can be stored in separate containers and mixed into a smaller storage container via a funnel (item B-ground up dog food, item C-ground up layer pellets, A-both dog food and layer pellets are added to a container via a funnel, then shaken.) The blended food container is used to fill the food dispensers and is large enough to store approximately 4 weeks supply.

5.4

- When food comes in moisture resistant packaging, tie off the opening as best as you can.

- Some stores purchase bulk quantities of produce then package them into smaller 5kg and 10kg clear bags. If food is purchased in clear bags, check that the food does not have any insects prior to purchase. Even one or two insects quickly become many thousands.

- Purchase good quality reputable brands which have good food handling practices.

5.5

- Individual ingredients remain fresh longer when stored separately. This reduces the risk of cross contamination with microbes/insects and problems associated with different moisture content. In effect if one product is infected with insects you haven't lost your entire batch, only the individual ingredient.

5.3 Wet Food- Nutrition and Processing

As outlined in previous sections wet food and moisture must be made available to cockroaches at all times to minimise cannibalism. If water is not freely available cockroaches will have no choice but to eat each other to obtain their moisture requirements.

Ideally food would be changed daily, however I have found that every second day is adequate if you have a water dispenser. The only exception to this are days of extremely high temperatures or humidity, which cause accelerated fermentation and therefore daily food additions may be preferential. If you choose to use fruit and vegetables as the sole source of water (no water dispensers) they will need to be added daily without failure.

Generally speaking vegetables are better than fruits as they don't ferment as quickly (high water content and sugars in fruits). I would recommend using apples and oranges which tend to ferment more slowly than other fruits.

Most vegetables can be used including, carrots, sweat potato, pumpkin, lettuce, broccoli, cauliflower, and beans). Root vegetables are superior to green vegetables as they contain a high nutrient/energy ratio and will generally last longer. The standard vegetable mixture I use are equal quantities of carrot and sweet potato due to their longevity, price and availability. I supplement this mix with other household leftovers. Vegetables to avoid include apple cores (seeds contain cyanide), avocado and citrus.

Many supermarkets are potentially a free source of wet foods as they throw away large quantities of produce on a daily basis. Most of the produce discarded is unsold produce, unsightly seconds, or off cuts (i.e. dirty outer folds of lettuce etc.). Staff tend to discard this material first thing in the morning and place them in small wheelie bins at the end of each aisle. This produce cannot be stockpiled out back due to legal reasons so you will need to pick up this material first thing in the morning.

Be cautious when using vegetables that are grown above ground as they are often sprayed with pesticides, which may kill your cockroaches if not washed. If vegetable scraps from the kitchen are used, it is advisable to wash the vegetables prior to putting them in the fridge using a water mixture containing 1 or 2 teaspoons of white vinegar per 2 litres). This is a good practice for yourself and your cockroaches as the acidic vinegar helps remove pesticides from the vegetables. Some vegetables such as broccoli, silver beet and cabbage contain high levels of oxalic acid, and their use should be minimised as they can cause health issues in reptiles and amphibians.

Small cricket colonies can be sustained by kitchen scraps alone, however larger colonies will need additional supplementation. As a general guide 2-3 carrots will feed a standard container described in Section 3.1 (Choosing a Container) every second day. This however will vary greatly depending on numbers and lifecycle stage.

Frozen foods

One quick and convenient method to top up vegetable supplies is to use frozen vegetables from the supermarket. Surprisingly frozen food can be cheaper than fresh vegetables, then these supplies are out of season. As they are snap frozen they preserve better than freezing your own vegetables which can become soggy when defrosted.

Another advantage of frozen foods is that pest insect species have been killed.

Freezing wet foods

When fresh vegetables are in season, they can be a cheap supply of wet food. To reduce preparation time I process large quantities using a food processor (with knife attachment) to chop the vegetables into large chunks (Refer to photo 5.6). Avoid using a grinder plate which shreds the wet food into a

5.0- Food and Water Requirements

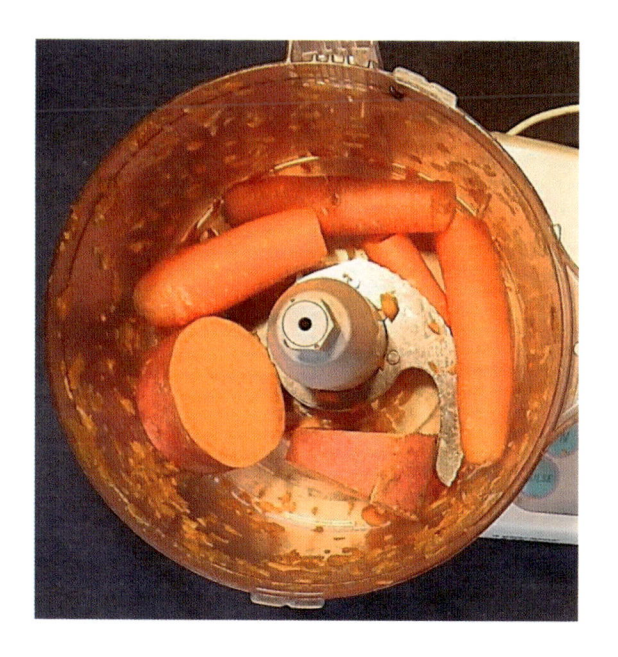

coleslaw consistency, as it ferments faster than larger pieces. The same principle applies to cutting kitchen scraps, larger pieces (approximately 4-5cm long) is better than finely chopped pieces.

The processed vegetables can then be placed into disposable take away containers and frozen for later use (Refer to photo 5.7 and 5.8). The freezing process reduces the quality of the fresh foods (become soggier) so if time is not limited fresh food is better.

The amount of food to be placed into each container will vary depending on the age and developmental stage of the cockroaches inside. Keeping a record of the amount of food added each week and recording it on a piece of paper on the lid (Refer to Section 9.6- Record Keeping) will ensure the correct amount of food is added without unnecessary waste.

5.6

Tip: If the fruits and vegetables placed into a food processor are roughly the same size, this will produce a consistent size pieces (Refer to photo 5.6).

Adding only just enough food which can be consumed at each feed will not only save you money, but prevent unnecessary fermentation and infestations of insect pests.

5.7

5.8

5.4 Gut Loading and Dusting

Gut Loading

Gut loading is a method of boosting the nutritional content of your cockroaches prior to feeding them to your animals. This is accomplished by providing them with high quality foods to boost their nutrient, energy and moisture levels. Your animals then benefit through ingestion of these enriched cockroaches. Animals that have been relocated, are ill or under stress may particularly benefit from gut loading and dusting.

Most pet stores that sell reptiles are likely to sell a commercially available gut loading formula. As you only use a small quantity this is a relatively cheap option. Alternatively you can make it yourself as outlined in Section 5.2 (Dry Food Recipe). It is recommended that you substitute lower grade foods (i.e. dog food) with higher grade kitten food which will generally have more animal proteins and higher fat content. A gut loading mixture can be mixed then stored into a separate container and used as required.

Providing energy rich fresh root vegetables (not frozen) such as carrot and sweet potato will also provide a good wet food gut loading option. Be sure to provide a good supply of water either through a water dispenser or fresh fruit and vegetables. Where possible feed the cockroaches gut loading foods at least 24-48 hours prior to feeding them to your animals. This will allow sufficient time for the uptake of nutrients and moisture.

Dusting

Dusting is a process to add a nutritionally rich powder to the outside of your feeder cockroaches. Again only a small amount is used so purchasing a commercially produced product is an economical way of adding nutrient to your animal's diet.

Place the cockroaches into a plastic "zip lock" bag or into a small high sided container (Refer to photo 5.9) and shake until the cockroaches are completely covered. Cockroaches should be fed to your animals immediately after dusting as they clean themselves on a regular basis.

Adding gut loading foods and/or dusting powders to your cockroaches are designed to "top up" nutrients and should not substitute feeding your animals a nutritionally balanced diet. If cockroaches are fed a high quality diet, then dusting and gut loading for the most part will be of secondary importance to your animals (with the exception of a few trace nutrients which can only be provided by dusting).

5.9

5.5 Feeding Cockroaches to Animals

Feeding cockroaches which are too large for a reptile can cause health issues such as compaction and choking. As a general rule, food no larger than the distance between the eyes should be fed to reptiles.

Releasing cockroaches in a controlled manner will prevent the cockroaches from escaping resulting in unwanted hygiene issues in the cage (detritus) or damage to your animals from nibbling body parts at night. Below are some techniques for capturing, temporary storage and releasing cockroaches in a controlled manner:

1) Cooling

Cockroaches that have been put into the fridge for approximately 5 minutes will be less active than cockroaches at room temperature. This will slow down their metabolism/movements and increase the capture rate for your animals. Placing them on a cool cement floor in cool months is a variation of this method.

2) Temporary Storage

This is my preferred method of temporarily storing live foods and feeding animals. The advantage of this system is that you only need to collect and filter your cockroaches once per week, and can easily access cockroaches at any time. It also allows detritus to be easily filtered prior to dusting. This system can be made by purchasing a container which will comfortably house cockroaches for a week. A 2L container will cater for a medium sized reptile for a week. A 5L container will cater for 2 or 3 reptiles.

Cockroaches can easily be removed via the feeding port by upturning and shaking into a tall dusting container or "zip lock" bag. Photo 5.10 shows the temporary storage container (left), tall dusting container and dusting powder (middle) and two meshed end caps (right).

Insert a feeding port into the lid using the same technique described in Section 3.8 (Making a Container). You will need two meshed end caps. One is kept unchanged with a metal mesh for ventilation

5.10

(ventilation port). The second end cap will need to have the metal mesh removed using tin snips and replaced with hydroponic plastic grid.

5.0 - Food and Water Requirements

5.11

The aperture on the hydroponic plastic grid is wide enough so that when you turn the container upside down (between 2-5mm), detritus falls through the screen, leaving only the cockroaches behind. Photo 5.11 shows container with normal metal mesh for ventilation (installed on left) and the second port used to remove detritus. Place chopped carrot in the container so the cockroaches have water and food whilst in temporary storage and replace every couple of days.

To collect your cockroaches, simply remove the ventilation port and shake the container contents into a tall dusting container, which has a similar diameter as the ventilation port (i.e. 90mm PVC piping). Once you have shaken out the detritus and cockroaches, place the "filtering port" over the dusting container and shake out the detritus leaving clean cockroaches. This process is shown in photo 5.12 and 5.13. Place your dusting powder into the container and shake. The cockroaches now are ready to be fed to your animals. At the end of the process place reattach the metal mesh end caps as cockroaches will eat the hydroponic mesh if left for long periods.

Tip: Remember to cut pieces of carrot prior to removing cockroaches, and add them after you shaken the container to remove the detritus and old carrot. In this way you have collected your cockroaches, cleaned the container and added new food at each harvest. No additional maintenance required!!

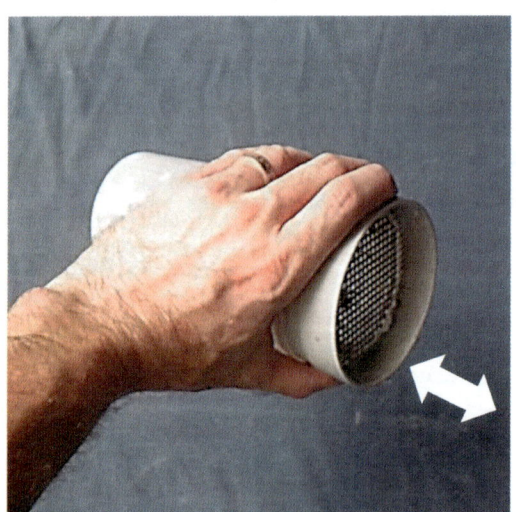

5.12   5.13

3) Egg Carton Structures

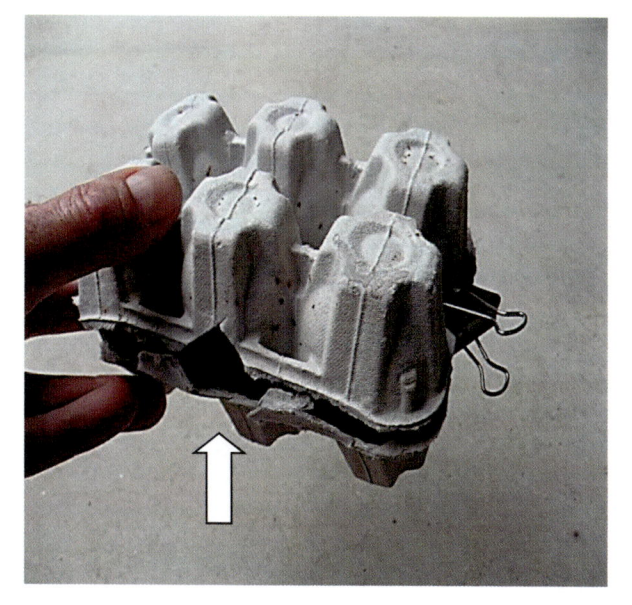

This is a useful way of removing a small quantity of cockroaches. These structures are made by folding an egg carton (one dozen) in half as shown in photo 5.14. The ends are held together using a bull clip or similar. Provide access into the egg carton by cutting access holes on the side as shown by white arrow in photo 5.14. Space can be made for the egg carton structure by cutting a corner from the large egg cartons in the containers and placing it into this gap.

Removal of cockroaches is a simple matter of removing the egg carton structures and shaking out the cockroaches into a dusting bag, animal enclosure or feeding box.

5.14

4) Box Container

As shown in photo 5.15, cockroaches are removed from the container, sorted and then placed into a separate container with the animal. This has the advantage that all cockroaches are consumed and you have no escapees in the animal's enclosure. A variation to this concept is placing the animal directly into the cockroach container where they can eat them directly.

5.15

5) Pipes

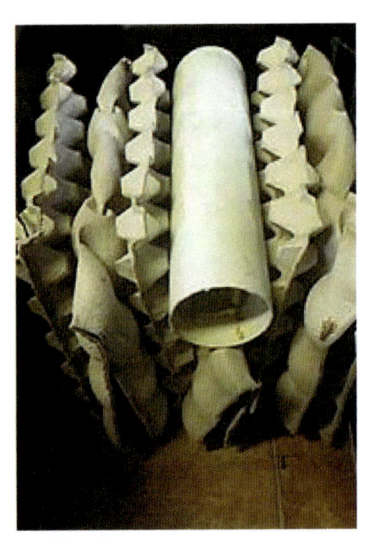

Place a section of 90 mm PVC plumbing pipe into the grow-out container with egg cartons on the inside. The animals will make their home in the piping and when you need cockroaches, upend the contents into a dusting bag or pipe filter to sort by size and to remove detritus (Refer to next section). The pipes can be easily fitted into the container by cutting the vertical egg cartons a little shorter so the pipe fits flush with the top (Refer to photo 5.16).

5.16

6) Pipe Filter

Once cockroaches have been removed from the container by a pipe structure (Refer to above), the cockroaches can be filtered using a pipe filter. This comprises of a section of 90 mm irrigation pipe with threaded irrigation caps at each end. As the pipes and pipe filter are the same size (90 mm irrigation pipe) they are able to connect into each other. In this way you can upend the contents of the pipe (cockroaches and detritus) directly into the filter without any escapees. The pipe filter has one end blocked off with a solid end cap so the cockroaches are contained in the pipe filter. Once you have disconnected the pipe (and placed back into the container) the second perforated cap is placed over the other end of the filter.

Photo 5.17 and 5.18 shows the components for the pipe filter as outlined below:

- A) 90mm plumbing pipe with threaded plumbing connections at both ends
- B) A funnel that fits into the 90mm plumbing ends. This can be made by cutting the top of a 1.25L soft drink bottle.
- C) Solid 90mm threaded end cap
- D) Holes drilled into solid 90mm threaded cap (filter)
- E) Base of a commercial cricket dispenser (Refer to next section)
- F) Lid to a commercial cricket dispenser

5.0- Food and Water Requirements

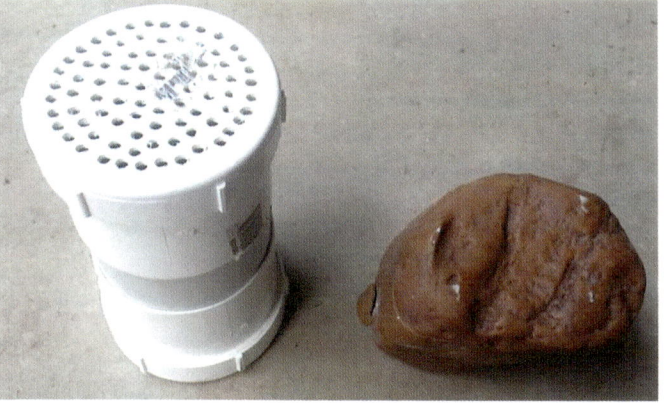

5.17

5.18

You can purchase a number of caps and drill various size holes to filter various sized cockroaches. (i.e. small holes if you have lizard hatchlings, large holes for adult lizards). Once you have filtered the desired cricket size (Refer to photo 5.19), you can insert the funnel into the top of the pipe filter and pour the cockroaches into your commercial feeder dispenser (Refer to photo 5.20) or directly into the animals container.

5.19

5.20

The Complete Cockroach Breeding Manual   Page 44

5.0- Food and Water Requirements

7) <u>Commercial Cricket Dispensers</u>

Photo 5.17 and 5.18 shows how a commercially available cricket dispenser is composed of two parts that clip together. Cockroaches are placed into the container and a plug is opened to allow the cockroaches out, one by one. As the animals are likely to sit in front of the plug hole where the cockroaches come out, few cockroaches ever escape.

As photo 5.21 shows, your animals (bearded dragon in this instance) will be very keen to pick off each insect as they come out.

<u>Feeder Cockroach Traps</u>

These are commercially available traps which attract unwanted cockroach escapes into a trap using bait. When they enter the trap they can be removed.

5.21

6.0 MAKING FOOD AND WATER DISPENSERS

6.1 Design Considerations for Food and Water Dispensers

Basic Food and Water Dispenser

A food feeder in its simplest form is a dish with wet or dry food placed in it. This is used by many people, however a food dispenser (with reservoir) has many benefits, and is best suited for efficient and large scale production.

Providing fresh food each day will provide cockroaches with food and a water supply, however it is very labour intensive.

Efficient Food and water dispenser

This has the following advantages:

- It is more cost effective as food is let out at a controlled rate and consumed on demand. Food is controlled to minimise wastage, and cockroaches are less likely to flick or move food from trays. Food flicked onto the floor creates hygiene issues.

- A food dispenser is more hygiene as fresh food is dropped in from above on regular intervals and does not stay long enough for microbes to develop.

- The food reservoir keeps the food fresher for longer as it reduces the surface area exposed to moisture (only the surface of reservoir is exposed to air).

- You can store large quantities of food in a dispenser and do not have to replace the dry food as often, which is useful for large colonies. If required you can add a larger reservoir if you plan to be away for extended periods (10-21 days). This good when you go away for holidays.

- As food and water is stored vertically in a reservoir, the dispenser can be more compact leaving more room for cartons and greater production.

- Water and food consumption peaks when cockroaches reach medium/large size and in the heat of summer. At these times food and water consumption is substantial for large numbers of cockroaches. A reservoir system is the only practical way to keep up with peak food and water consumption.

Cockroaches will drown in open water so water containers need to have material placed over it to allow cockroaches to climb out. Nylon washing scrubs is a good option as it is very robust, can be used over and over, and is easily cleaned using a high pressure hose. Other materials such as sponge and cotton wool can be used but generally need to be thrown out regularly, as they can harbour bacteria or degrade over time. Pebbles are another good option as they are easily washed and reused. Some people use water crystals as a water source; however I have found this method to be unreliable as it can be eaten by the cockroaches or evaporates in high summer temperatures and needs to be continually monitored. They are also difficult to clean from containers when they dry out.

The systems developed below are applicable for the containers and breeding systems I have chosen for my own purposes. Each person will have different containers, components and breeding strategies, however the instructions given below are designed to provide you with examples which can be adapted to your own circumstances.

6.2 Food Dispenser- Small Scale Production

As outlined in Table 11 a simple small scale food dispenser can be made by adapting a bird feeder purchased from your pet store (Refer to photo 6.1). As you are working with a purchased product, the volume of the feeder cannot be changed and may be suited only to small numbers of cockroaches. This is a basic design which is useful for one or two containers, however if you plan to have more containers the "Large scale food dispenser" (Refer to next section) may be more applicable.

Table 7- How to Make a Small Scale Food Dispenser

Construction Method	Photo
1) Cut the sides of the bottom tray with tin snips to a lower height that allows easy access for cockroaches. 2) As many bird feeders are designed to be off the ground and attached to a cage, they often have angled bottoms which prevents them from sitting upright on the ground. To make an even base, add resin putty (used to block pot plant holes) purchased from your hardware store, to the back of the feeder. 3) It is common for cockroaches to crawl from the bottom tray up into the food reservoir getting trapped and dying. Place an ice cream stick into the container to allow cockroaches to crawl out of the food reservoir (Refer to photo 6.1).	6.1

4) The food opening at the bottom of the plastic tube will need to be made smaller as cockroaches will flick all the food from the reservoir onto the floor until emptied. Reduce the food opening by:

   a) Cut a small rectangular piece of plastic (for example from a take away container lid) the width of the feeder and cut out a 1cm square rectangle from the middle (Refer to photo 6.2). This cut section will allow a controlled amount of food to the cockroaches.

   b) Place the piece of plastic in the front of the feeder so it restricts the food (jam between reservoir and front plastic) as shown by arrow in photo 6.1.

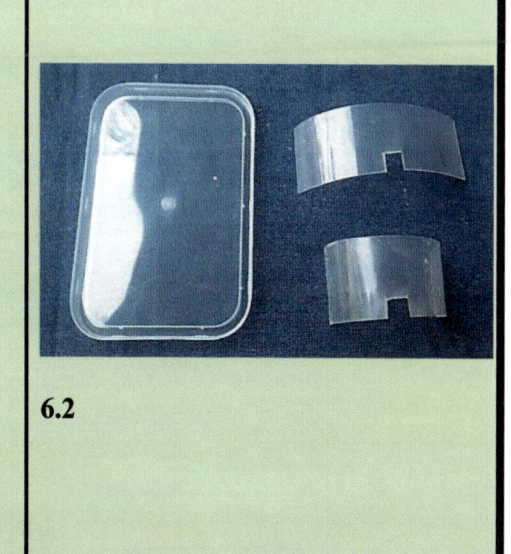

6.2

6.3 Food Dispenser- Large Scale Production

Purchasing a bird feeder as described in Section 6.2 (Food Dispensers- Small Scale Production) costs around $10 (Australian) from a pet store and they have a fixed and limited reservoir capacity. This may be sufficient for a small set-up or containers with less than 400 cockroaches, however is often not suited to a larger commercial sized colony which house 500 or more cockroaches per container.

Below are instructions to make cost effective food and water dispensers which can store larger quantities of food suitable for containers housing 500 or more cockroaches. They are inexpensive to make, durable and are stable (do not spill when moving the container for cleaning). The design is compact with both the food and water containers fitting into a small food tray.

<u>Making a Food Tray</u>

As outlined previously, the food tray allows for water and wet/dry foods to be removed together. Table 8 demonstrates how to make a food tray which holds the water and food dispensers.

Table 8- Making a Food Tray

Construction Method	Photo
1) Purchase a long narrow container which fits the width of your container as shown by the bottom tray in photo 6.3. The tray must have sufficient gaps along its vertical sides to allow access to the food for the cockroaches. 2) Cut some of the vertical supports with metal snips to allow greater access for cockroaches. Retain enough support so the container can be lifted without collapsing. In the trays shown above, every second vertical support is retained for support (Refer to top tray in photo 6.4). The spaces created in the middle section of the tray will act as handles for lifting the tray out of the container 3) If the food/water dispensers do not quite fit the trays, you can cut out sections so the trays overhang as shown with arrows in photo 6.3 and 6.4. 4) I suggest making extra trays to replace dirty trays during cleaning.	6.3 6.4

6.0- Making Food and Water Dispensers

Large Scale Food Dispenser

Table 9 demonstrates how to make a large scale food dispenser.

Table 9- Making a Large Scale Food Disperser

Construction Method	Photo
1) COMPLETED LARGE SCALE FOOD DISPENSER This dispenser comprises of the following components (Refer to photo 6.5). A) Food reservoir- holds dry food. B) Connecter- joins the food reservoir with the base. C) Base- holds food to be eaten by cockroaches. D) Food restrictor- controls the amount of food that is released from the reservoir. This is located on the inside of the connector and is shown by a line indicated by the arrow. Subsequent sections will show in better detail.	6.5
2) DISPENSER BASE a) Choose a small rectangular container (approximately 300ml), available from most supermarkets (Refer to photo 6.6). Disposable containers will suffice and they are relatively easy to cut.	6.6

The Complete Cockroach Breeding Manual

b) Cut the container as shown in photo 6.7. The front end of the base can be cut to a height of approximately 12mm so cockroaches can easily enter the feeding tray. This height is sufficient to prevent food from spilling and being kicked out by cockroaches. The sides that will attach to the joiner can be cut higher (15-20mm) so the tubing is supported and has something for the silicon to bond to.

6.7

3) CONNECTER

c) Purchase large clear plastic tubing from a hardware store. The tubing used in the dispensers shown in photo 6.8 is 55mm in diameter.
d) Cut a section of the tubing using a hacksaw approximately 5cm long (Refer to photo 6.8).

6.8

e) Place the clear tubing into the container tray at the high end. Using flexible silicone, attach the tubing to the container. Be sure to fill in all gaps underneath and to the back of the tubing to prevent food and cockroaches from being trapped (Refer to photo 6.9).

f) Using tin snips, cut a 15mm square from the bottom of the tubing to allow food through. In later sections the amount of food that is released from this hole will be controlled with a food restrictor (Refer to arrow in photo 6.10).

6.9

The Complete Cockroach Breeding Manual

g) Hold the tubing in place whilst the adhesive is drying with tape (Refer to photo 6.10).

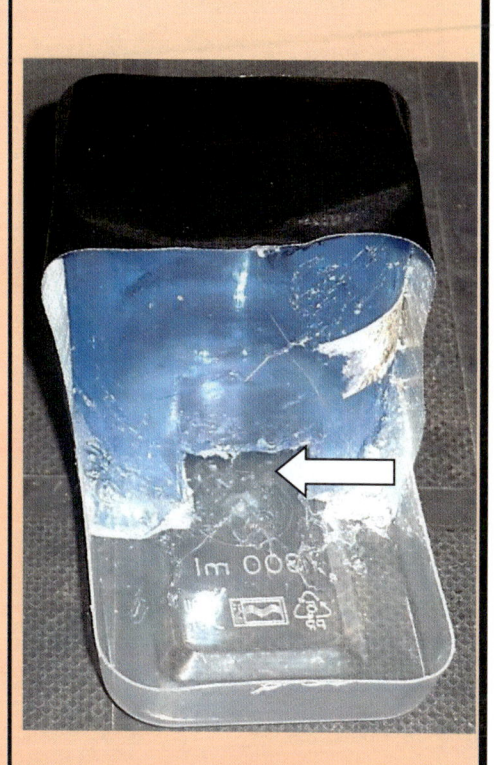

6.10

4) **FOOD RESTRICTER**

h) The food opening at the bottom of the clear tubing will need to be narrowed to prevent cockroaches from flicking the food out of the reservoir until it is empty. Using the lid of the disposable container used for the base, make a "food restrictor" by cutting a rectangular piece of plastic from the lid of the container used for the base. From this section of plastic cut a 1cm square as shown in photo 6.11. This will be used to restrict food from escaping out of the reservoir in an uncontrolled way.

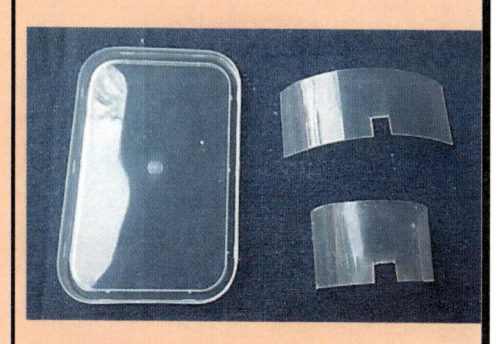

6.11

6.0- Making Food and Water Dispensers

i) Bend the piece of plastic into a "C" shape (Refer to item "A" in photo 6.12) and place it into the connecter as shown by the arrow.

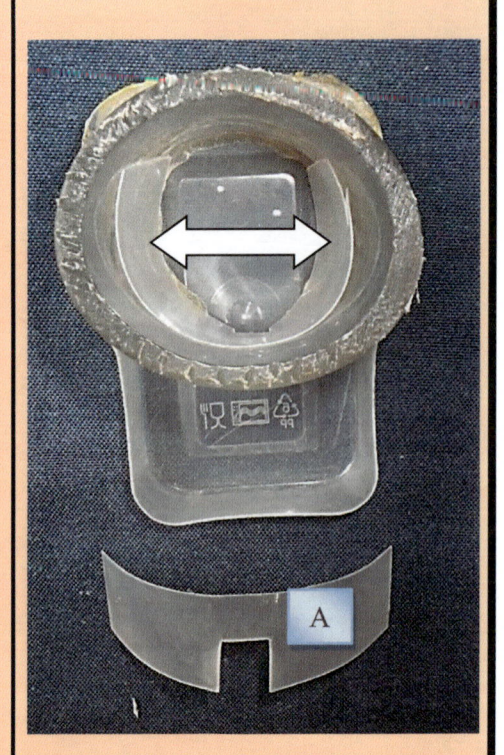

6.12

5) RESERVOIR

j) Choose a drink container that has a circular/conical neck that will wedge into the clear tubing (Refer to photo 6.13). A 400-500 ml juice container should hold enough food for around 500-600 cockroaches for a week (In Australia the Berri brand orange juice works well).
k) Cut the thread off and the bottom of the drink bottle as shown in photo 6.13.

6.13

6) FITTING COMPONENTS TOGETHER

l) After the adhesive has set, fit together the pieces of the feeder. Push the reservoir into the plastic tubing and fill with food.

m) Note the food restrictor is placed on the inside of the tubing and bent in the shape of the tube (Refer to photo 6.12 and arrow in photo 6.14 showing the line which food restrictor is placed internally).

n) Place a paddle pop stick into the top to allow cockroaches which dig their way into the reservoir to escape. Fill the dispenser with food and place onto the food tray and the food dispenser is ready for use.

6.14

Water dispenser

The following water dispenser has the advantages of providing water for over a week, is cheap to produce and is stable so they don't fall over when moving containers. Table 10, demonstrates how to make a large water dispenser.

6.0- Making Food and Water Dispensers

Table 10- Making a Large Scale Water Dispenser

Construction Method	Photo
1) COMPLETED LARGE SCALE WATER DISPENSER As shown in photo 6.15 the dispenser comprises of the following main components: A. Reservoir- holds water B. Tray with vertical connector (Refer to arrow). An elastic band connects the water reservoir to the vertical connecter. C. Nylon dish washing gauze- prevents cockroaches from drowning.	6.15
2) TRAY AND VERTICAL CONNECTER a) Choose a small rectangular container (approximately 300ml), available from most supermarkets (Refer to photo 6.16). Disposable containers will suffice and they are relatively easy to cut. Get a container with a "lip" shown by the arrow in photo 6.16, as this will be used to grip the elastic band.	6.16

The Complete Cockroach Breeding Manual

b) Using a ruler, mark a line around the bottom of the container approximately 15-17mm from the bottom. This is the line which marks the top of the food tray. This depth is sufficient to prevent spillage whilst moving tray for maintenance.
c) Draw two vertical lines 1cm apart from the centre of the container as shown in the container at the top of photo 6.17.
d) Use the lines marked above cut the shape shown in the tray at the bottom of photo 6.17.

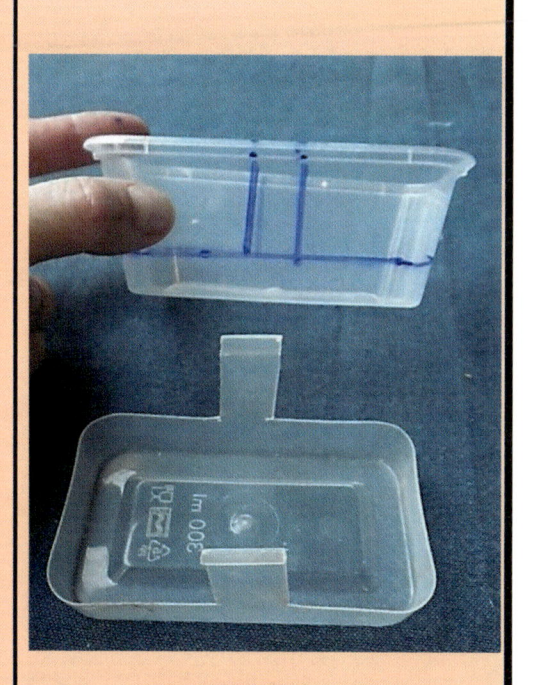

6.17

3) NYLON GAUZE

e) Place a nylon dish washing gauze insert in the tray to prevent the cockroaches from drowning. Using a marker draw the outline of the base of the container onto the gauze.

f) Cut this shape out. Fold in half and then cut a thin slit (3mm wide) from the centre of the gauze as shown in photo 6.18 and 6.19. This will create an air gap under the water reservoir releasing the vacuum and allowing water to come out.

6.18

g) To be effective the slither needs to be longer than the width of the bottle neck (i.e. 5mm on either side). Don't make the slit longer or wider than necessary, as cockroaches will try to burrow into it and drown in the reservoir. Arrows in photo 6.19 indicate the width of the slit.

6.19

The Complete Cockroach Breeding Manual

6.0- Making Food and Water Dispensers

h) Once you have accurately measured and cut gauze for the tray, use this as a template for the rest of the containers (marked with a "T" in photo 6.18 and 6.20).

Tip: You can reduce the frequency of cleaning by cutting extra gauzes for the base (i.e. cut four gauzes for each container to reduce cleaning frequency by a quarter or once per month)

6.20

4) WATER RESERVOIR

i) Purchase a plastic and transparent drink/fruit juice/milk bottle as the reservoir. The bottle will need the following requirements:
    - Hold a minimum of 400-500ml of water which is the volume required to water more than 500 large cockroaches over a week.
    - A "rill" or indentation around the bottle which allows an elastic band to be placed around the bottle which attaches the tray to the reservoir (Refer to bottom arrow in photo 6.21 and photo 6.22). The rill needs to be at the correct height so that when you place the reservoir into the tray, it matches the height of the vertical connector of the tray. This distance is shown by the two arrows in photo 6.22.
    - So that the container has greater stability during movement, purchase a bottle with a wide opening (at least 25mm wide) and preferably with a wide flange.
    - In Australia the brand of bottled fruit juice which fits the above requirements is "Berri, fruit juice containers, 400ml) as shown in photo 6.21.

j) Using a hacksaw, cut the neck of the juice container at the threaded neck of the bottle, to expose the flattened flange (Refer to photo 6.22, top arrow).

k) Cut two pieces of plastic inserts (i.e. Insert used for drilling into brick walls) at opposite ends. Silicon the inserts into the rill, opposite each other using clear silicon. This is used as a grip to pick up the elastic band from the rill during cleaning (Refer to red inserts in photo 6.22, left arrow).

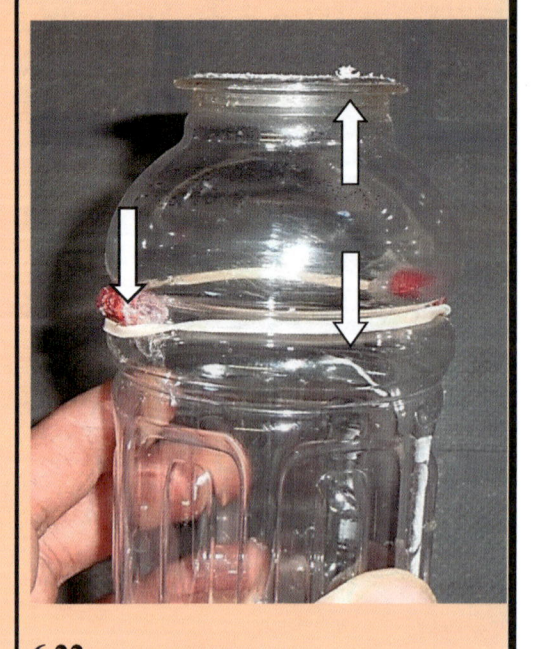

6.21

6.22

The Complete Cockroach Breeding Manual — Page 57

5) SETTING UP WATER DISPENSER

l) Place a thick elastic band around the "rill" and hook it under the edge of the vertical connecter of the base (Refer to arrow in photo 6.23). In Australia a common brand of elastic band is "Superior, size no 28" which can be obtained from stationery outlets and newsagents. Try to purchase a thick elastic band for strength and durability, at least 2-3mm wide.

m) Set up the water dispenser as shown in photo 6.23.

6.23

Water Dispenser Using Pebbles

An alternative to using nylon dish washing gauze is pebbles. Using pebbles instead of gauze has cleaning advantages. For instance, half a bucket of clean pebbles may last many months for small scale operations, and the dirty pebbles can be put aside and cleaned within a few minutes for re-use.

Medium size aquarium gravel is a good pebble to use as it's easily cleaned and non-porous and unlikely to absorb nutrients or bacteria. The process for making a water dispenser with pebbles is essentially the same process as outlined above for a gauze system with a few minor changes which are outlined below in Table 11.

The Complete Cockroach Breeding Manual

6.0- Making Food and Water Dispensers

Table 11- Making a Large Scale Water Dispenser with Pebbles

Construction Method	Photo
1) COMPLETED LARGE SCALE WATER DISPENSER- WITH PEBBLES As shown in photo 6.24 the dispenser comprises of the following main components: A) Reservoir- holds water B) Tray with vertical connector (Refer to arrow). An elastic band connects the water reservoir to the vertical connecter. The lip at the top of the vertical connector holds the elastic band (Refer to arrow). C) Pebbles substrate- prevents cockroaches from drowning.	6.24
2) RESERVOIR AND TRAY a) Make a water reservoir and water tray using the same method described above in Table 10 (Making a Large Scale Water Dispenser). b) The depth of the water tray will in most cases be the same as outlined in instructions above for a gauze tray system. If however you get excessive spillage you may need to make the trays a little deeper to allow for sufficient depth of gravel c) Using a hacksaw cut two notches in the lip of the water reservoir, which will allow water to escape when placed in the water tray (Refer to arrow in photo 6.25). Start with a small notch that is only a few millimetres in depth, and make them deeper if required (ie water has trouble coming out).	6.25

The Complete Cockroach Breeding Manual

3) SETTING UP WITH PEBBLE SUBSTRATE

d) The water reservoir is set up in a similar manner to the gauze system however it varies slightly as outlined below:
- Fill the reservoir with water by tap or upturning it in a bucket of water.
- Place reservoir on the bench with the opening facing up.
- Place an empty tray upside down on top of the reservoir opening, as shown in photo 6.26.

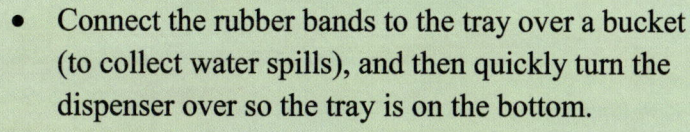

- Connect the rubber bands to the tray over a bucket (to collect water spills), and then quickly turn the dispenser over so the tray is on the bottom.
- In the bucket, place gravel into the tray so that the surface is moist (Refer to photo 6.27). The tray is ready for use.

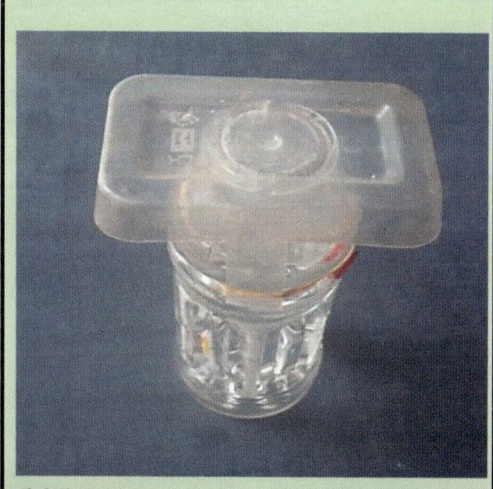

6.26

6.27

7.0 HEATING AND STORAGE

7.1 Heating and Humidity Requirements

Heating

Heating is an important factor which influences the growth rate and life span of cockroaches. In general terms, the higher the temperatures, the faster the growth rate and shorter the lifecycle. Table12 provides a guide to temperature ranges for cockroaches:

Table 12- Temperature Ranges for Cockroaches [1]

Cockroach reactions	Temperature (Centigrade)[1]	Comments
Cold stress for prolonged periods	Below 10-20 degrees (50-68 degrees Fahrenheit)	Cockroaches can live below this temperature for short periods; however will struggle or die over longer periods.
General growth	20-25 degrees (68- 77 degrees Fahrenheit)	Slow to average lifespan
Minimum temperature for productive breeding	25 degrees (77 degrees Fahrenheit)	
Optimal growing temperatures,	32-35 degrees (90-95 degrees Fahrenheit)	Fast growth rates, reduced life expectancy.
Heat stress	38 degrees or greater (100 degrees Fahrenheit)	Survival is dependent on ventilation and providing sufficient moisture

[1] **Note that temperatures described in Table 12 are based from internal container temperatures from a tropical environment and variations may exist in different climates. Figures are based on Speckled Cockroaches (Nauphoeta cinerea), slight variations will be found between different species.**

As shown above, cockroaches can survive a range of temperatures, however optimal grown is found in a relatively narrow temperature range (32 to 35 degrees Centigrade). Productivity and breeding consistency will suffer away from these preferred temperature ranges. In the heat of summer I have had container temperatures exceeding 40 degrees Centigrade with no deaths, however during these periods I had good ventilation, plenty of available water and fans blowing through the containers.

Humidity

Humidity requirements vary between species, however most tropical species prefer a medium to high humidity (60-75%). Refer to section 2.3 (Species Selection) for humidity requirements for the species you are keeping. Cheap humidity meters can be purchased from most pet stores.

As outlined in earlier sections humidity/moisture is often obtained from a water source (i.e. water dispenser) or wet foods. Humidity is important to prevent dehydration and to facilitate molting. Once a cockroach has lost its old protective exoskeleton, it is prone to dehydration. Where cockroaches are dying during their molt, humidity should be increased.

Too much humidity can create harmful pathogens such as fungi, bacteria and mites. Condensation on the walls of the container is a sign of too much humidity or poor ventilation. Your egg/apple cartons will also quickly become floppy/soggy, food becomes mouldy or ferments which results in bad smells.

Humidity generally increases as moisture availability and ambient temperatures increases, and decreases with reduced water availability and lower ambient temperatures.

Humidity can be increased in the following ways:

- Partially block off the ventilation ports with tape.
- Cover the whole ventilation port with a thin towel
- Add free available water sources source such as a bowl with pebbles, in it so cockroaches don't drown or a small substrate area which is misted every few days. The larger the surface area, the more humidity will evaporate.
- Provide daily wet foods to your cockroaches
- Mist and spray the sides of the container every 2-3 days.

Humidity can be decreased in the following ways:

- Increase ventilation
- Remove unnecessary water sources such as substrate, additional water bowls etc.
- Is the amount of wet foods provided excessive?

7.2 Heating Systems

As outlined above, a heat source during cold weather conditions is an essential component to a productive breeding colony. Every person will have their personal preference when it comes to choosing their heating method. Below are various heating systems to provide you with the various options to heat cricket containers:

Heat Mats

My preferred heating method for small/medium scale production is heat mats (Refer to photo 7.1) for the following reasons:

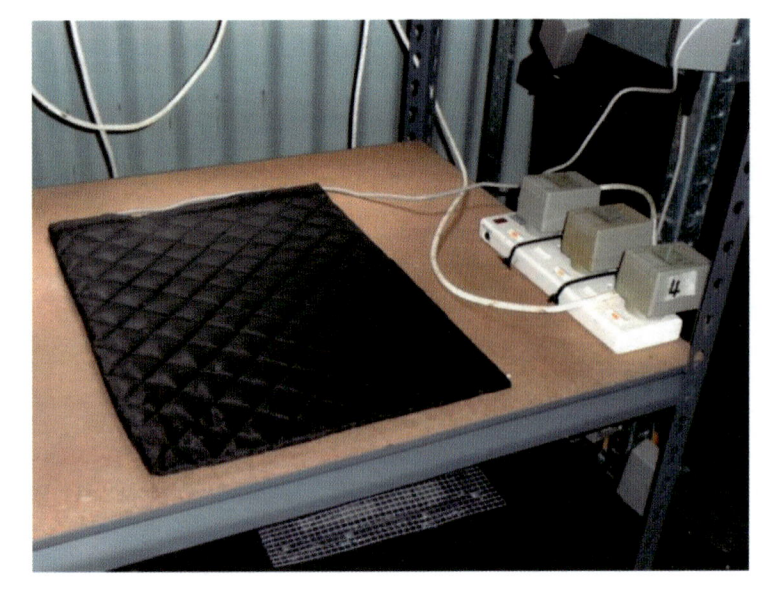

7.1

- The container can be removed from the shelf to undertake maintenance without getting tangled in cords. This is particularly applicable with containers which are stacked above each other on shelves.
- Heat levels can be adjusted quickly by flick of a switch (purchase models with variable temperature switches).
- They are a diffused heat source which spreads heat across the whole container and moves from the bottom to top.
- As they produce localised heat they are a good option if you have a multi-use shed/room, that you do not want to heat the whole area (i.e. is used as a storage and a cricket breeding area).
- They are efficient as nearly all the energy is converted to heat and not light (a light source would need to be 70-90W equivalent, 40-45W required for heat mat).

The only drawback to heat pads is that they are relatively expensive to purchase (around $40-70 Australian) and are best suited to small to medium size colonies. The internet now has a range of cheap heat pads to choose from. For the 70L containers described in Section 3.1 (65cm long by 42cm wide) you will need as a minimum 40-45W rated heat pad for a temperate environment (mild to cold climates). Very cold climates (i.e. with snow) may require higher rated heating devices in winter. You can get away with a 35-40W rated heat pad in tropical environments. You may be able to reduce the costs of purchasing heat pads by approaching a large wildlife rescue organisation that purchases them in bulk.

Tip: The transformers of heat pads can be heavy, particularly when many are placed onto a single power board. Secure top heavy power boards to the shelf by drilling holes in the shelves and using cable ties to secure the power board (Refer to photo 7.1).

Heat Coils

Heat Coils are a long plastic coated coil (like a long rope) which can be placed underneath the breeding container. If you can't afford heat pads, heat coils are a good alternative. The Coil can be placed in a zig zag configuration to get even heat distribution. The coil can be kept into position by tying it into position (using cable ties) on a metal grid. The advantage of heat coils is they are cheap and adaptable. For the 70L containers described in Section 3.1 (65cm long by 42cm wide), as a minimum a 45-50W rated coil, 6m long, would be sufficient for a temperate environment (mild to cold climates). Very cold climates (i.e. with snow) may require higher rated heating devices in winter. You can get away with a 40-45W rated heat pad in tropical environments.

Heat Lamps/Heat Emitters

A heat lamp is an incandescent light bulb, and a heat emitter is a ceramic bulb. The advantage of a heat emitter is that it is more robust, will last longer, and more heat efficient. The disadvantage is it is more expensive.

Many people have used heat lamps successfully and they can be made relatively cheaply when compared to purchasing heat pads. For safety reasons you should purchase heat lamps from a pet store or get a qualified electrician to install larger systems. Personally I have not found heat lamps/heat emitters to be very user friendly and they are not my preferred heating method for the following reasons:

- Cords are connected to the lid which gets in the way during harvest and maintenance activities
- There is an inherent fire and electrical risk associated with making and operating them
- You need to replace the bulbs on a regular basis to regulate the heat output between seasons.
- They are a point source of heat which creates heat gradients within the container.
- Heat source comes from the top. As heat moves in an upward direction, heat does not effectively penetrate the lower sections of the container and heat is lost through the lid.
- Are not as energy efficient, as some of the energy is used to produce light.

Element Heaters

For large commercial facilities the most cost effective method of heating large numbers of containers is to heat a room/shed using thermostatically controlled heaters. Various options are available including electrical, radiator/ceramic heaters or reverse cycle air conditioner/heaters. Always be aware of fire hazards when using element heaters.

Heat and Electricity Regulation Devices

Thermostats can greatly reduce your energy needs by turning off heating devices when the desired heat has been reached. Conventional switch thermostats, turn off the whole heat device once the desired temperature is reached. Dimming thermostats, increase or decrease the electricity to a heat source which reduces the heat output proportionally. Dimming thermostats are more expensive (around $100-110 Australian) however they save more electricity, and increase the life of heat sources. Heat bulbs in particular, last longer as they are not switching on and off all the time, which reduces the bulb expanding and contracting with heat.

Another useful device is a *"Master/Slave" power board*. This is a power board with say 6 electricity ports, one of which is a master switch and the other 5 are slave switches. If electricity is cut to the master switch (by a thermostat for instance) then it tells all the other 5 switches to turn off. Conversely is power is reinstated to the master switch, the other 5 follow. This allow you to run 6 heat pads/coils/bulbs from the one thermostat.

Solar Air Heaters

This is an innovative system which holds good potential to inexpensively heat large rooms for free during the day. There are many different designs but the principle is generally the same, the sun heats an enclosed metal box and the hot air rises to the top and is extracted via a solar powered air extractor. A relatively small unit can produce large amounts of heat, even in cool temperate environments.

Commercial units can be expensive, however the internet has many sites which give DIY instructions to build inexpensive solar air heaters using scrap roof tin and guttering materials. The air pump will need to be linked with a thermostat to prevent them from overheating the cockroaches in hot weather and to activate heaters in cold periods or at night. The great advantage of solar heaters is that your heating for half the day is free, and they can heat large rooms which would normally be expensive. This reduces the expense associated with heating from pad/light heating systems. For further information, search "Google" and "U tube" under the heading of "solar air heaters" for DIY instructions and books to build solar air heaters.

Solar Panels

Cheap solar kits (panels, inverter and batteries) can be purchased from solar and hardware stores to produce enough electricity to run large numbers of heat pads etc. For instance an $80 solar panel can run approximately 7 heat bulbs (100W each). This technique has the potential to eliminate the heating costs reptile enclosures and cockroach/cricket breeding heat pads.

7.3 Reducing Heating Costs

Thermodynamic Principles

Heating can be a significant cost associated with cricket production. Heating costs can be reduced by working with nature and the following basic thermodynamic rules:

- Heat travels in an upward direction.
- Heat moves from areas of high temperature to areas area of low temperature.
- The greater the temperature difference between two areas (i.e. inside and outside the container), the greater the heat loss or gain.
- Heat loss is reduced as insulation increases.
- Heat can be gained by placing an object adjacent to a heat source or heat sink (e.g. brick wall, chimney).

- Reducing temperatures by just a few degrees can result in great reductions in heating costs. For instance reducing the operational temperature of a reverse cycle air conditioner/heater by 1 degree can reduce operating costs by around 10%.

Heating costs can be reduced by implementing the following location and efficiency considerations:

Location Considerations

Place the colony adjacent to or within the following locations:

- Next to heat sources such as fireplaces, ovens, hot water heating systems or clothes dryers.
- Against heat sinks (stored heat) such as brick walls which store heat during the day and release it at night.
- Next to a closed window that is exposed to sunlight. An open window can create drafts which removes heat.
- An existing heated reptile room.
- The warm side of a house/shed.

Efficiency Considerations

Below are additional ideas to reduce heating costs:

- Depending on the type of heater in use, thermal gradients may develop in a room (i.e. containers close to or far away from the heater, higher temperatures near the ceiling, and cooler temperatures near the floor). Fan forced systems may help to reduce thermal gradients.
- When using heat pads, place insulation foil and towel (towel to be placed between insulation and container) under the containers to prevent heat being radiated away from the containers.
- Place a towel over the top of the breeding containers in winter to reduce heat loss.
- Use passive heating (solar heaters) to heat rooms up during the day and use other heating systems during cooler periods and at night.
- Use thermal and reflective insulation in the room or shed cockroaches are housed.
- Use switch and dimming thermostats (Refer to Section 7.2- Heating Systems) to regulate temperature so excessive heat is not generated. In summer it may be possible to turn off your heaters all together.
- If you can't afford thermostats, use timers to turn off heat sources during the warmer parts of the day.
- To reduce the number of timers of thermostats you need to buy, place a number of heat pads onto a "Master/Slave power board" which is connected to a single thermostat/timer (Refer to Section 7.2- Heating Systems). Check that the power board is able to handle the electricity load being placed on it.
- Use efficient heating systems such as heating pads (refer to above sections)
- Turning off the heater when cockroaches get to the desired size. This will prevent them from getting larger than desired, increase their shelf life and reduce food and energy costs.

7.0- Heating and Storage

- For containers which are stacked above each other, reduce the heat settings for containers on the top row as heat rises and warms containers.
- Close any curtains and blinds in a room.
- If heating a room, get a system that is efficient for its size. Small heating systems that try to heat large rooms run at sub-optimal rates which increase energy consumption.
- Store cockroaches at least 0.5-1m off the ground as cold air will sink to the floor.

7.4 Estimating Heating Costs

It is important to know your heating expenses to determine production costs. Below is a method to estimate the costs associated with heaters:

1. <u>How much do you pay for your electricity (i.e. dollars/kilowatt hour).</u>

    This can be obtained from your last electricity bill. If you have both peak and off-peak rates, you will need to break down number of hours for each rate.

2. <u>What is the energy consumption of your heater (i.e. no of kilowatts/hour)</u>

    If you are using a 1000W heater, then the appliance uses 1 kilowatt every hour. The energy consumption rate can be obtained from either the back of the appliance, user manual or manufacturer's website.

3. <u>How many hours do you use the heater per time period.</u>

    For instance to work out how many hours are used per month, determine how many hours the heater is on per day and then multiply it by the number of days in a month.

Below is a formula and example to estimate the total cost of a heater over a month:

| Hours used per month | X | Rated power of heater in kilowatts (kW) | X | Cost per kilowatt hour (kW/H) | = | Total electricity cost per year ($) |

Example- 40W heat mat, operating 0.7 of the time with thermostat and warm summers.

| 728hrs/month | X | 1kW= 1000W 40/1000 (0.04kW) | X | 0.3272 kW/H (Australian figures) | = | $9.52 by 0.7 (operating 0.7 of the time with summer) = $6.66/month |

With the recent interest in energy consumption due to global warming issues, there are a number of energy meters that can be purchased or borrowed (environmental product stores, energy companies) which directly estimates the energy cost of appliances.

As an additional check, compare your previous electricity bills (prior to heaters being installed) with recent bills (with heaters installed). Make sure you compare a similar time period from the previous year, as energy consumption differs from winter to summer.

7.5 Managing Excessive Heat

The management of excessive heat is an important consideration for sheds and hot aspects of houses, particularly in summer. I have had cockroaches survive temperatures greater than 40 degrees however at these temperatures they would be stressed and productivity reduced. If temperatures exceed 38 degrees Celsius, it is recommended to reduce temperatures. Some suggestions are provided below:

- Place thermal or reflective insulation on the roof of the room/shed (roof batts, reflective paint or reflective foil).
- Place a fan in front of the colony which turns on and off via a timer or thermostat. As outlined in Section 3.3 (Ventilation) a well-designed container will facilitate fan forced air through a container.
- A more expensive option which may be viable for a colony in a spare room is thermostatically controlled dual heating/cooling systems.
- Remember to turn off heat sources or set them to lower settings in warm times of the year (Summer) and warm times of the day (from early to mid-afternoon).

7.6 Storage of Colony

There are a number of shelving options available to store a larger colony:

Commercial Storage Systems

Shelving stores supply commercially available stacking systems. They are expensive however they can be pulled apart, allow storage all the way to the roof and have wheels which allow them to be moved. This allows for easy sweeping and cleaning.

Bracket Shelving

The most cost effective way of making shelving along walls is an adjustable wall storage system as shown in photo 7.2. These systems can be purchased from your local hardware and comprises of two vertical rods which attach to the wall, and shelving brackets. They are fully adjustable and the shelving comes in a variety of lengths. A variety of materials can be used as shelving including, fibro/cement sheeting, ply board, timber or old doors.

7.2

Flat Pack Shelving

The other option is flat pack shelving (Refer to photo 7.3). These can be expensive and I have found they are fairly limited in their ability to add shelves or shelving heights. One advantage they do have is they are a good option when you need to place containers in the middle of a room or shed.

7.3

8.0 MAINTENANCE AND PEST MANAGEMENT

8.1 Maintenance

Regular maintenance of a cricket colony is required to prevent bacteria and fungal infections which can cause disease or productivity loss. Many of the automated feeding and water systems in this manual will help minimise time spent feeding and undertaking maintenance. Maintenance activities are summarised in Table 13 and as outlined below:

Table 13- Maintenance Schedule

Frequency of activity	Activity description
Every second day	- Add wet foods
Once per 7-10 days (or as required)	- Refill or replace dry food reservoir. - Refill water reservoir and replace nylon pad/pebbles. If densities are low this can be extended to once per fortnight. - Review food uptake and note new amounts on container tag. - Remove detritus from bottom of container
Once per month (or as required)	- Review temperature settings - Clean components (i.e. supports, screen food/water dispensers)
End of harvest or every 6-9 months which comes sooner.	- Replace cartons - Clean container and all components
Once per 12 months	- Add new stock to improve genetics

1) Adding Wet Goods

- Every second day wet food needs to be provided.

2) Replacing Food and Water Dispensers

- Typically done once per week for high densities, however this can be extended to once per fortnight for lower densities.
- In warmer and humid weather, wet foods can ferment after a few days.

3) <u>Removing Detritus and Cartons</u>

- Cartons need to be replaced once they are excessively soiled or are being eaten. With the Cartons lifted up off the soiled floor, they will last much longer, up to 6 months (or as required). Dirty cartons, waste water/food and detritus can be placed in the garden as mulch or placed into a mulch bin or composer. The combination of water, cardboard and waste material makes an ideal compost material which breaks down quickly.
- Removal of detritus needs to be undertaken once you can't see the bottom of the container. This is typically the same frequency as adding water to the substrate (i.e. once every week or two).

4) <u>Cleaning Used Containers/Dispensers</u>

- Clean and wash out the container and 6-9 months or as required.
- Wash and spray the container with a mixture of water, washing detergent and disinfectant (e.g. ammonia, Milton's baby disinfectant or melaleuca/eucalyptus oil).
- Water dispensers in most cases will need to be replaced weekly however if relatively clean can last two weeks. Dry food dispensers and food tray will normally last for two or more weeks. If the dry food reservoir is relatively clean then it may only need to be refilled.
- If you prepare multiple dispensers/components etc., you can get away with cleaning once per month.

Tip: One way to prevent escapees when doing maintenance is to open the container in open sunlight or bright lights so they move to cartons for cover. Additionally the activity of cockroaches can be reduced by placing them in a cold area or cement floor for a few minutes. This is most effective in cooler periods.

5) <u>Adding Cockroaches to Breeder Container to Improve Genetics (All Systems)</u>

- Once or twice every 12 months add cockroaches to improve genetics (Refer to Section 8.4- Genetics).

Tip: Where you are operating a larger commercial operation, you may wish to spread larger maintenance activities (i.e. cleaning containers/components) progressively over the year. For instance if you have 8 containers operating, you will need to clean one container/month if each container is to be cleaned every 8 months. Another tool is to make a timetable to help organize your weekly/yearly maintenance activities.

8.2 Cleaning

Small scale cleaning can be done in a normal manner with a brush and tap. However if you have multiple containers, the below tips will stream line the process. With the method described below, it should take approximately 3-4 minutes to replace food, water and removal of detritus

Replacing Food and Water Dispensers

Cleaning food and water components are described below in Table 14.

Table 14- Cleaning Food and Water Dispensers

Cleaning Method	Photo

1) CLEANING COMPONENTS
 	
a) Obtain a shallow rectangular cleaning tray as shown in photo 8.1. To one side (left hand side in photo) place the following dry food/cleaning items (from top to bottom):
 	
   A. Cleaning tray (blue in colour)
   B. Small food container with dry food mix.
   C. Additional dry food.
   D. Small bucket to place waste dry food with spatula to scape food.
 	
b) To the other side (right hand side in photo) place the following wet food/cleaning items (from top to bottom):
   E. Bucket of water
   F. Small bucket to place waste water
   G. Spare water trays and nylon gauze or pebbles
 	
c) The blue tray, contains any food or water spills from cleaning activities, and also contains any stray cockroaches that escape from the food/water trays. Within the blue tray place the following items as shown (from top to bottom in photo):
   H. Container of fresh wet food
   I. Funnel (top of a 1.25L soft drink bottle) to place dry food into dispensers.
   J. Small disposable 300ml containers to scrape detritus from breeding containers (Refer to photo 8.9).
 	
d) Remove the food tray from the container by gripping the rails in the middle and lifting. Hold the tray over the container for a few seconds to allow cockroaches to climb out, before placing it into the cleaning tray. Place barrier cream along the top rim of the blue maintenance tray.
	8.1

8.0- Maintenance and Pest Management

e) Any cockroaches that remain will be retrieved from the cleaning tray if they escape (Refer to photo 8.2).

8.2

2) CLEANING WATER DISPENSER

f) Place water dispenser over the waste water bucket and unclip the elastic band so that the tray and gauze fall into the bucket draining the waste water (Refer to item" F" in photo 8.1 and photo 8.3).

8.3

g) Fill a new water reservoir by submerging it into a bucket of water (Refer to item "E" in photo 8.1 and photo 8.4) or using a tap. If the reservoir is not soiled, you can reuse the same container over a period of two or three weeks.

8.4

The Complete Cockroach Breeding Manual

8.0- Maintenance and Pest Management

h) Place the filled water reservoir on the bench with neck upright (so water does not flow out) and place the tray and gauze centrally over the neck of the bottle as shown in photo 8.5.

i) Where pebbles are used in the trays instead of nylon gauze, the same principle applies; upturn the water tray so that the pebbles fall into a bucket, drain waste water, place a new tray on top, upright the tray and fill it up with pebbles. For further details refer to Table 11 (Making a Large Scale Water Dispenser with Pebbles).

8.5

j) Use the plastic tabs on the bottle to grip the elastic bands, and pull it over the rib of the water tray (the vertical connectors). With the elastic bands secured, turn the bottle over and place it on the bench so the tray is supporting the bottle. Dip the tray into the bucket filling it with water, then tipping it slightly to run off excess water (Refer to photo 8.6). The water dispenser is now ready to be placed in the food/water tray.

8.6

3) **CLEANING FOOD DISPENSER**

k) Cockroaches will pollute the food tray with detritus as they feed. Pick up the food dispenser and scrape out the waste food from the tray into the dry waste bucket. Remove the Food/water tray and scrape off any dried/fermenting food into the food/waste basket. This tray can be re-used over a period of a few months without needing cleaning (Refer to photo 8.7 and 8.8).

8.7

The Complete Cockroach Breeding Manual

l) Once both the food and water dispenser have been replaced or refilled, place them onto the food tray along with the wet food. The food tray is now ready to be put back into the cricket container.

8.8

Cleaning Detritus from a Container

Method for removing waste is described in Table 15.

Table 15- Removing Detritus

Cleaning Method	Photo
1) SIMPLE METHOD a) Tilt the container so that one end of the container collects the faeces/waste. Using the trellis basket described in Section 3.7 (and photo 8.10), lift the cartons off the ground, tilt the container and the detritus will collect at one end. b) Make a "waste collector" by adapting two small disposable plastic containers (same trays used for the water dispenser- (Refer to photo 6.6) by cutting the sides as shown in photo 8.9.	8.9

The container on the left has low sides and is small enough to get into any tight corners and can be used to scrape waste to a corner. The container on the right has high sides on one side so that it can collect larger quantities of waste once it has been pushed to a corner (Refer to photo 8.10).

8.10

2) CLEANING MULTIPLE CONTAINERS

c) Another method of collecting detritus is to transfer all the cartons into a second empty container (cleaning container) using the trellis basket
d) This will leave the container empty and you can easily scrape up waste. Once finished you return the cartons and shake the cleaning container over the container to return any escapees (Refer to photo 8.11, white arrow shows cockroaches to be returned).
e) Scrape the detritus into one corner and use the plastic "waste collectors" to remove them to the dry waste bucket (Refer to instruction "B" above).

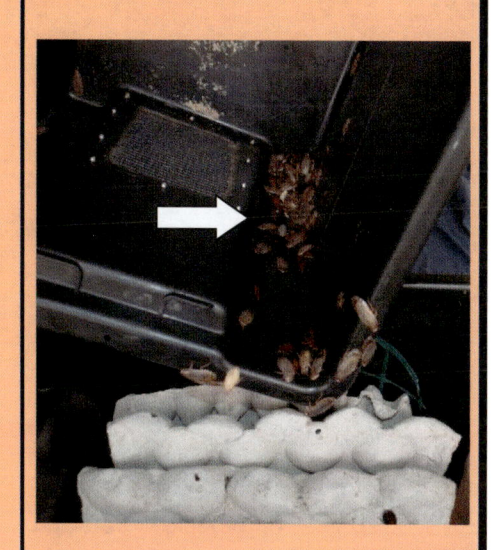

8.11

f) If the faeces contains small cockroaches that you want to retrieve, place the waste into a shallow tray placed on top of the carton (Refer to photo 8.12). By the time you have made up the food/water tray the small cockroaches will have jumped off the tray back into the cartons leaving the faeces behind for disposal into the dry waste container. Try to keep the trays on the cartons as long as possible so that the smaller cockroaches have the greatest opportunity to jump back into the container.

8.12

g) Replace the cartons and water/food dispensers/trays back into the container.

Cleaning Components

Below are some tips to help with the cleaning process for multiple containers:

1) After replacing food from the containers, dirty components will need to be cleaned. Separate out the different components (i.e. gauze, dispensers, food containers) to streamline the cleaning process. A quick way of separating out the items is to place each different cleaning item into a separate bucket as you do your maintenance.
2) Pre-soak items with stubborn stains such as wet food containers/trays, and gauze. Items which are very soiled (i.e. water dispenser gauze) are best soaked on their own so they don't contaminant cleaner items.

8.13

3) Using a high pressure hose or tap, clean the components. Many sheds do not have sink facilities and a simple cleaning station can be made with three outdoor chairs as shown in photo 8.13. Dirty pre-soaked items are placed in the container on the left, with the cleaning done in the middle container using a high pressure hose and clean items placed into the container on the right. To reduce overspray whilst cleaning, spray the components into a bucket with holes drilled into the bottom (or use your 20L cricket filtering bucket). To prevent your cleaning area getting saturated, place a large bucket under the middle chair (as shown by arrow) so that waste water from the spraying falls through the bucket holes into the collection bucket below (chairs are pervious to water- i.e. meshed). Once it fills up discharge into the garden or to water plants. In most cases loose dirt/grime can be removed with just hosing, however stubborn stains can be scrubbed off with a bucket of soapy water and a brush.

4) Cleaning with normal soapy water or water with dilute vinegar are good cleaning agents. Stubborn stains not removed by spraying can be removed by spraying them with a detergent and tea tree oil (as an antibacterial agent) and then scrubbed using a stiff brush. Most components only need to be hosed or scrubbed, however the water bottle gauzes and the breeding trays should be sterilised. A good sterilisation product to use is "Milton's" which is a baby bottle

8.14

The Complete Cockroach Breeding Manual

cleaning product. This product is effective at killing microbes whilst being soft enough that it won't affect cockroaches.

5) Place a mesh bag (laundry clothes bags) into a bucket and fill with water. Place the sterilising product into the water, and place the items into the laundry bag (Refer to photo 8.14). Once they have soaked for the desired time you can remove and drain the items by lifting the bag from the bucket. You may need to replace the bucket with fresh water and repeat the process to remove any sterilising liquid residue (Refer to product instructions). Remove the items once again with the bag, shake off excess water (or twirl bag through the air) and hang to dry in the sun for additional sterilisation (Refer to photo 8.14).

6) Medium sized items (food/water dispensers, trays, funnels etc.) can be placed into large laundry clothes bag for drying or you can make a larger draining bag using trellis mesh as shown in photo 8.15. This can be made by cutting a long rectangular section of garden trellis and fold it over into a "U" shape. The sides of the trellis bag (shown with arrows) can be joined using fencing "C" clips and a crimper used for fencing.

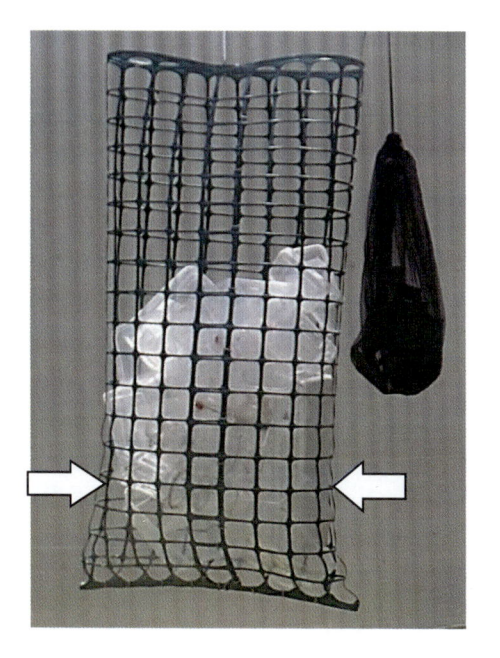

8.15

Tip: If you plan to wash items such as water dispenser gauze and trays in an infrequent basis (i.e. make duplicates and wash once per month) it is recommended to give them a quick rinse on the day they are remove. This will remove the bulk of the waste and prevent them putrefying between cleans.

7) Very large items such as containers, lids, buckets, blender components etc., can be placed onto drying racks such as an old security door screen. An object can be placed at one end to create an angle for better drainage. Remove any old fly screen to improve air flow (Refer to photo 8.16).

Tip: Large items can be cleaned on an elevated outdoor table to reduce back strain.

8.16

8.3 Pests

As cockroaches are an excellent source of protein, nutrients and water, there are many animals and microorganisms which will take every opportunity to eat your cockroaches. Potential pests include ants, spiders, foreign cockroaches, geckoes, rodents, bacteria and fungi.

The larger pest species are effectively controlled by a quality lid and screen system as outlined in Chapter 3.0 (Container Design and Construction).

Diseases

All animals will contract diseases where basic husbandry requirements are not met and their immunity is reduced. With the techniques in this book you will be able to do basic cleaning and provide food/water with minimum maintenance. This will improve the health and reduce diseases.

Other sources of diseases can be accidently introduced when you bring in new animals from the pet store (particularly to improve genetics see later sections). Carefully inspect the new animals to make sure they don't have genetic defects or small parasites. Genetic defects such as deformed wings or body parts are a sign of disease or inbreeding and these animals should be avoided.

Where a disease has been introduced and taken hold, the best method is to start over fresh, and sterilise the containers and components with bleach or disinfectant. Bring in new cockroaches from a reliable and good quality source.

Ants

Ants can be a major threat to a colony as they are able to, co-ordinate quick and attack within minutes or hours. They can be hard to control as they can be small enough to bypass many lid systems or through holes in your screening. Unless adequate measures are put in place they will consume all your cockroaches and will continue to do so until you have an adequate barrier.

Below are some measures which may help to prevent or reduce ant attacks:

- Regularly check the perimeter of your shed or cricket storage area to prevent an attack before it has started. Initially ants will send a couple of "scouting" ants to locate a food source which tell the rest of the colony where the food source is.

- Destroy the nest and ants with sprays. Hardware stores have a variety of sprays including; perimeter sprays (ants crawl over them and die), contact sprays (spray ants and ant trails) or nest/queen targeted poisons (ants ingest food and take it back to nest/queen). The best places to spray are the colony nest and ant trails leading from the colony, and around the perimeter of your ant colony (i.e. shed or door and window entrances etc.). Other products include baits/lures and baited dust/granules.

- Ants generally do not like to travel across open ground. If you have trees or plants growing up against your shed/house, mow or poison the perimeter and cut overhanging trees to reduce their cover. This also has the added advantage of allowing you to see an ant trail when it appears.

8.0- Maintenance and Pest Management

- Do not throw out old food and detritus waste near your cricket colony (i.e. into the garden next to the shed door or house). This waste food will attract ants which will then locate your colony nearby.

- If containers are on shelving which is not connected to the wall you can place the feet of the shelving in a shallow dish of water with liquid soap. Many ants have the ability to walk on water, however the liquid soap reduces the surface tension of the water and the ants drown.

- If the above fails then talk to your local government agricultural department and ask for a taxidermist to identify the type of ant which is causing the problem. Once you know what type of ant they may be able to suggest an appropriate methodology for its control. If all else fails contact a professional pest controller who have experience in ant control.

- Electrical cords leading to the stands (heat pads/thermostats etc.) must be safeguarded by making "ant guards' through placing sticky insect paper (i.e. cockroach sticky pads) around the cords as described in Table 16.

Table 16- Making an Ant Guard for Power Cords

Construction Method	Photo
a) An ant deterrent can be made from a cockroach glue pads, which are commonly used to control cockroaches and other pests (Refer to photo 8.17). They can be purchased from hardware or shopping centres.	8.17

8.0- Maintenance and Pest Management

b) Cut a 10cm square piece from the pad and then cut along the blue line shown in photo 8.18. At the middle (shown by a blue T shape line) cut a central hole to allow room for the power cord to pass through.

8.18

c) Pull the electrical cord to the centre by sliding it through the side cut (Refer to photo 8.19).

8.19

d) Sticky tape the two halves together on the non-sticky side (back), so the sticky pad surrounds all of the electrical cord (Refer to photo 8.20).
e) Remove the protective cover over the sticky pad to activate the sticky sections. Ants will now have great difficulty getting past the cord to the cockroaches.

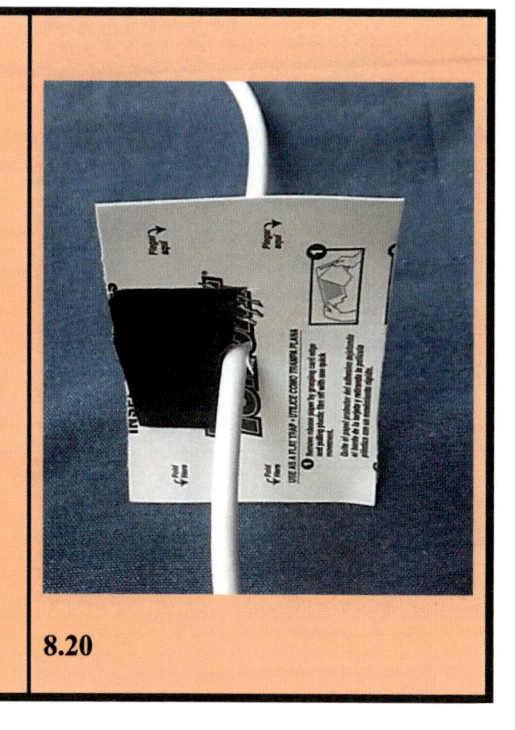

8.20

Spiders/Cockroaches

Spiders and foreign cockroaches can accidentally be introduced into a container through cardboard cartons or through ineffective lid systems. Foreign cockroaches will quickly make their selves home and can outcompete the desired species. When you place cartons into the container, inspect them for pests and remove unwanted hitch hikers.

Another source of spiders/cockroaches is the trays and tubs used in maintenance. They often reside in these areas as they take advantage of any stray insects from the previous activities. Inspect all trays/tubs prior to use and remove them by brushing with a dust pan brush.

8.4 Genetics

As you will be recycling new cockroaches from the grow-out containers back into the breeder containers, overtime the genetic diversity of the colony will reduce. If this persists it may create problems such as reduced productivity, resistance to disease and genetic defects (damaged wings, deformities).

To minimise these effects it is recommended to add new fresh stock to your breeding containers once or twice a year to maintain genetic diversity. Try to use as many different suppliers as possible to maximise different strains as some commercial supplies may also have genetically restricted gene pools.

8.5 Safety

All forms of animal farming have potential inherent biological risks associated with pathogens and microbes, however when appropriate measures are taken these risks can be minimised. Below are examples of ways to reduce potential risks, however it is the responsibility of the operator to take a full risk assessment of their working environment and take the necessary safety precautions.

IF IN ANY DOUBT AS TO THE CORRECT OR SAFE PROCEDURE TO FOLLOW FOR ANY ACTIVITIES DESCRIBED IN THIS BOOK SEEK PROFESSIONAL ADVICE.

- Always follow manufacture's operating instructions and observe safety precautions when using equipment and or materials described in this book.
- Ensure no objects are placed near or against any heaters to prevent fires.
- Wear disposable gloves when handling unhygienic products such as detritus, waste food/water, cockroaches, substrates or cleaning activities. Gloves are to be used when you have open cuts or sores.
- Wash your hands carefully after handling cockroaches or detritus, and use a nail brush to remove dirt from under the nails. As an added measure you may wish to use a waterless alcohol sterilising gel.
- Following handling of materials which are soiled or dusty activities, a shower is recommended.
- Wash hands using liquid soap dispenser and not a soap bar to reduce secondary contamination and sterilizing gel.
- Shower after cleaning activities.
- Avoid eating or smoking after cleaning activities
- Avoid washing hands in the kitchen sink, use an outside or non-food preparation skink (i.e. laundry)
- Use appropriate dust masks when dealing with dusty products such as detritus, grinding dry food, substrate mixes, cleaning activities.
- Use safety ear plugs/muffs to protect ears from noisy machinery (i.e. grinders, food processors etc.)
- Have adequate ventilation in work areas to remove odours and dust.
- Regularly clean or disinfect benches, floors, containers and components
- Use soap and disinfectants when cleaning containers and components.
- All electrical work should be undertaken by appropriately trained electricians.
- Cover any wire or sharp objects on containers or work areas.
- Use correct lifting handling techniques when lifting heavy or awkward objects. Avoid twisting movements, particularly under load.
- Provide adequate training on safety procedures for all staff or volunteers.
- Never allow unsupervised children access to the area or equipment.

9.0 GRADING AND SELLING
9.1 Grading by Size

Grading is the process of sorting cockroaches into various size categories (i.e. small, medium, and large), usually for harvest.

A suggested method to count and grade cockroaches is described below in Table 23.

Table 17- Grading Cockroaches

Counting and Grading Method	Photo
1) FILTERING COCKROACHES a) The easiest way to grade large quantities of cockroaches is by filtering. This can be easily achieved by drilling holes into the bottom of a bucket, which allows small cockroaches to fall through to a "collection bucket" below (no holes in it) and large cockroaches are left in the top "filtering bucket". b) This is shown in photo 9.1 ("A"- bottom collection bucket, "B"- top filtering bucket, "C"-lid with inbuilt metal funnel). For small quantities of cockroaches a 5L bucket is sufficient, for commercial quantities a 20L bucket is required. c) Photo 9.2 shows a close up view of the underside of the lid with a metal funnel. The lid is placed onto the top of either buckets (collection or filtering) and allows you to invert the bucket and shake the cockroaches into a container for harvest. The metal funnel is made from a plumbing connector available from a hardware or plumbing store. A hole can be cut into the lid to place the funnel, by tracing the shape of the funnel on top of the lid, drilling a pilot hole, and using tin snips cut out the hole. As shown in this photo, the bottom of the connector has a flange which can be attached to the underside of the lid using silicon adhesive.	9.1 9.2

d) Try to source buckets which have an internal "lip" about one third from the bottom of the bucket. When one bucket is inserted into another, it rests on the lip leaving a gap at the bottom. This gap will prevent the filtered cockroaches being crushed by the bucket above. If you are not able to locate a bucket with an internal lip, you can achieve the same effect by placing a block of wood on the bottom of the collection bucket so the top filtering bucket rests on the block.

e) If you require a range of different sizes, you will need a different bucket for each size category. Photo 9.3 shows cockroaches that have been filtered.

9.3

2) TRANSFERRING COCKROACHES

f) Photo 9.4 shows a good bucket type which allows for the easy storage and transfer of cockroaches due to its internally fitting lid and spout.

9.4

g) Alternatively, large 20L "baby nappy buckets" also make a good temporary cricket storage containers once cockroaches have been filtered. Transfer of cockroaches to other containers is made easier by cutting a hole in one section of the lid (Refer to photo 9.5) to allows cockroaches to be tipped out for weighing. The first bucket shown in photo 9.4 is preferable as the spout prevents escapees when pouring cockroaches.

9.5

The Complete Cockroach Breeding Manual

9.0- Grading and Selling

Tip: *Cockroaches and crickets can be easily removed from the container for filtering by placing the cartons into a large clear vacuum storage bag (Refer to photo 9.6 and 9.7) and tapping the carton against a hard surface to dislodge cockroaches. Once all the cockroaches have been collected, they can be tipped into a temporary storage container using a large funnel.*

9.6

9.7

9.0- Grading and Selling

Tip: When placing a carton into the plastic bag, have the carton and bag opening along the same alignment (both placed vertically) so that the cartons easily slide into the bag. (i.e. have bag and cartons in the same direction as shown with arrows in photo 9.8) To capture escapees, the vacuum bag can be placed in a spare container during the transfer of the cartons from the container into the bag (Refer to photo 9.8- i.e. spare container on left side, with bag in it).

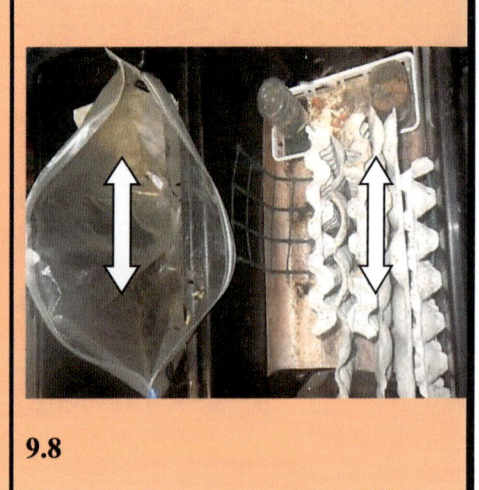

9.8

9.2 Estimating the Number of Cockroaches

<u>Smaller Quantities</u>

Smaller quantities are usually purchased from a pet store in small take away style containers (Refer to Section 9.3- Packaging and Transport). Although not stated on the container the quantity of cockroaches per container is by weight (i.e. one carton of cockroaches is approximately12g or approximately 30-35 large cockroaches). The advantage of selling smaller quantities is that they sell for a higher price. This can offset the extra time it takes to package individual containers.

As explained in the above section (large quantities), providing a set weight of cockroaches will avoid inconsistencies with providing a set number of cockroaches with slightly different sizes. Initially it is necessary to purchase a number of containers from your local pet store then weight and count the cockroaches to get a handle on how many grams are sold by your competitors.

The same process of measuring and recording the weight of cockroaches can be used as outlined above in the larger quantities section. As you are only interested in the weight, you won't need to do the formula calculation which works out the number of cockroaches. For small clients I do a standard package of three containers for "X" dollars. If someone only wants one container I will prepare a small container, however if they want three containers I have found it easier to place all the cockroaches (i.e. three containers by 12grams = 36 grams plus 15% extra = 14g in total) into a single calico bag or zip-lock bag (see below sections). This avoids the more time consuming process of packaging individual containers.

<u>Large Quantities</u>

Large quantities of cockroaches (more than 100-200 cockroaches) are most commonly sold as a set number of cockroaches (for example $65 for 1000 cockroaches). Customers often do not know how cockroaches are measured and each person will have their own perception of what is value for money. For example some people will think that more cockroaches in the container is better value, whilst others

The Complete Cockroach Breeding Manual

will think larger cockroaches is better value. This can result in a perception problem when the customer sees slightly different sized cockroaches or different quantities of cockroaches between each visit.

To avoid confusion or disappointment, it may be beneficial to explain that the quantity of cockroaches is determined by weight and the size or quantity of cockroaches will vary slightly for each batch. To help explain the concept I use the analogy of a 45g packet of potato chips. Each packet of chips may have slightly different size chips on average (smaller chips if packet has been shaken), however each packet will have the same weight of chips and hence are of equal quantity and value.

The best way to estimate the number of cockroaches for larger quantities is outlined in Table 18:

Table 18- Counting Cockroaches- Large Scale

Counting and Grading Method	Photo

A) MATERIALS
 	
a) Photo 9.9 shows the equipment needed to measure cricket as labelled below:
 	
   A. Electronic scales
   B. Large clear smooth sided plastic container to hold cockroaches whilst weighting. (i.e. plastic biscuit containers) Paint an insect barrier cream on the top of the container to prevent escapees as described in earlier sections.
   C. Small clear plastic container to store cockroaches that have been counted. Paint an insect barrier cream on the top of the container to prevent escapees as described in earlier sections.
   D. Large funnel with end cut off to make the opening wider. This will prevent a cricket bottleneck which results in them escaping.
   E. Cricket counting device (Refer to instruction "B" below for instructions how to build)
 	
b) Filter the cockroaches to obtain the desired size as outlined in Section 9.1 (Grading by size).
	9.9

B) COUNTING METHOD c) Count 30 individual cockroaches and place them into a small plastic container using a funnel (Refer to photo 9.9, item "C".	

Cockroaches can be counted by hand however this often results in escapees or inaccurate counts.

d) If you are counting cockroaches on a regular basis, you can make a "cricket counter" by modifying an "car oil refilling container" from a car supplies store (Refer to item "E" in photo 9.9).

As shown in photo 9.10, a cricket counter can be made by placing a 25cm section of 12mm clear piping (item "C") into the opening of the funnel lid (item "A"). A joiner between the funnel lid and the clear piping can be made from a short section of irrigation pipe, which is jammed between the two parts, and secured with silicon (black section in photo 9.10). The counter is operated by placing a hand full of cockroaches into the counter (via the funnel) and tipping the counter so that cockroaches move through the clear tubing. You can then count the cockroaches individually in a controlled way as they fall into a clear container (Refer to item "B", photo 9.9). You can adjust the speed they come out by adjusting the angle of the counter.

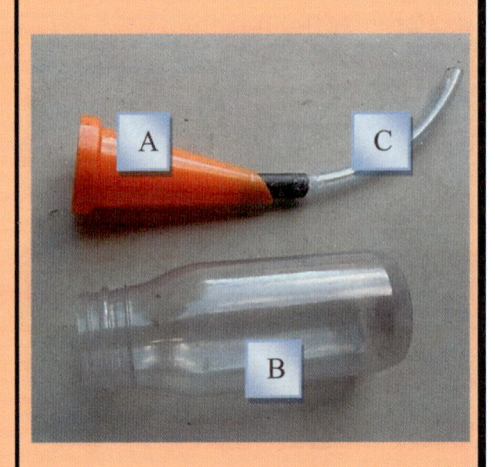

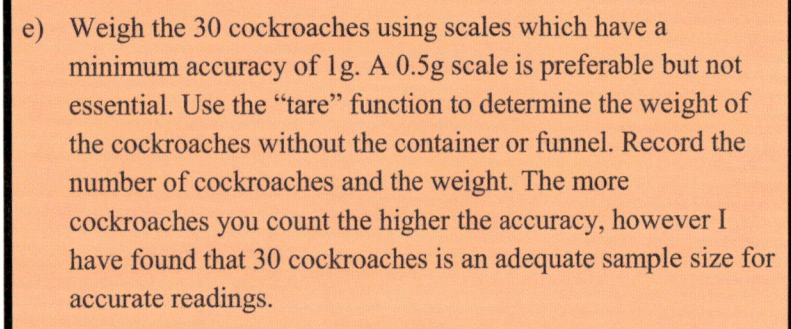

9.10

e) Weigh the 30 cockroaches using scales which have a minimum accuracy of 1g. A 0.5g scale is preferable but not essential. Use the "tare" function to determine the weight of the cockroaches without the container or funnel. Record the number of cockroaches and the weight. The more cockroaches you count the higher the accuracy, however I have found that 30 cockroaches is an adequate sample size for accurate readings.

These figures will be used to work out how many cockroaches you have as outlined below.

f) Place the 30 cockroaches you counted back into the container holding all the cockroaches to be harvested. Weigh all the cockroaches to get a total weight.

Tip: Cockroaches can be transferred into containers by tipping them into a funnel placed into the top of the container (Refer to photo 9.11). The funnel can be left on top to prevent cockroaches from jumping out.

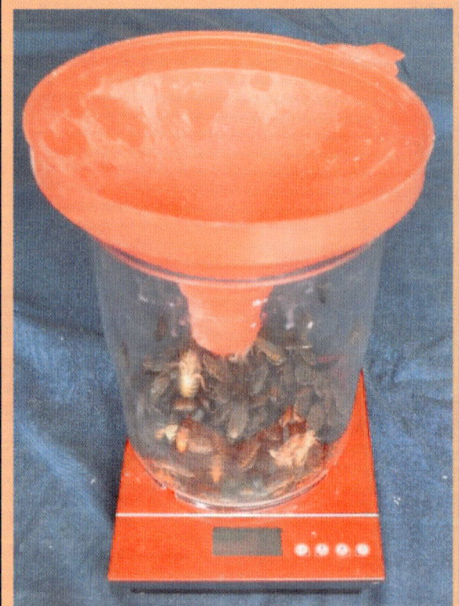

9.11

To transfer cockroaches from this container to another container or calico bags for transport, invert the funnel and tip the container upside down as shown in photo 9.12.

9.12

C) CALCULATIONS

g) I recommend providing an additional 10-15% extra to account for measuring inaccuracies, death and to provide an incentive for people to get their cockroaches from yourself.

h) Divide the total weight of 30 cockroaches into the total weight of all the cockroaches, and then multiply by 30. This will give you the total number of cockroaches in the batch as shown in the below formula and the example provided below:

Total number of cockroaches = (Weight of total cockroaches ÷ Weight of 30 cockroaches) × 30

i) Below is an example to demonstrate the above formula:

- 30 large cockroaches weigh 12.6 grams.
- The total amount of cockroaches in your container is 475grams.
- Divide 12.6 into 475g which equals 37.7.
- Multiply 37.7 by 30 cockroaches, which equates to 1131 individual cockroaches.
- It is recommended to provide all of the 1130 cockroaches in an order for 1000 cockroaches to provide an additional 10-15% to cover for inaccuracies and possible deaths.

j) At each harvest record the weight of the 30 cockroaches and the volume (ml) of cockroaches in a large measuring jug for each size category. If you keep good records, eventually you will be able to estimate the number of cockroaches by placing them into a measuring jug to get a volume. This will negate the need to do the whole weighing process.

9.3 Packaging and Transport

Once the cockroaches have been graded and weighed, the next step is to package them for transport. The longer the cockroaches spend in their temporary transport containers the higher the mortality rate. You will need to explain to your client, that the cockroaches must be kept in a cool spot out of the sun during transport. If cockroaches need to be transported in hot weather or over long periods, place the containers/bags into an esky with ice packs on the bottom. Do not seal the esky so tightly that it prevents all ventilation. Table 19 outlines methods to transport cockroaches. As you progress from option one to three below, the amount of cockroaches you can package/transport increases:

Table 19- Transport Methods

Transport method	Photo
A) SMALL CONTAINERS (SMALL QUANTITIES) This storage system is the same used by commercial suppliers of cockroaches to pet stores. The take away containers can be purchased from kitchen and food supplies stores or for small quantities you can use old take away containers from home. This set up consists of the following: • Small 750ml plastic take away containers with holes drilled into the lid. Larger numbers of lids can be done at the same time by placing half a dozen on top of each other and setting the drill on slow to reduce cracking (Refer to photo 9.13- left top and left bottom). • Place egg carton inside, and approximately 5mm of hydroponic vermiculite or course sand to absorb odour and moisture. • Place small pieces of chopped carrot on top of the cartons for moisture and food. Cockroaches can be transferred to the container by cutting a hole in the lid of a container so a funnel can be placed through the lid (Refer to photo 9.14). Once the cockroaches have been poured into the container via the funnel, simply replace the lid with the hole with a normal lid. This can be done by placing both lids end	9.13

to end and sliding the lid with the hole past the container so the normal lid slides over the top without any cockroaches escaping.

Note that most large producers will not put more than 12g into a container to prevent overstocking and higher mortality rates. Most commercial operations need to factor approximately 2 days transport, 3-4 days on the shelf in the pet store and then 7 days with the client (nearly two weeks), so higher densities are not feasible. As you are selling directly to the public, you won't have this problem and can provide 15% more (14g) without problems and they will be fresher and last longer than your competitors.

9.14

B) LARGE ZIP-LOCK BAGS (SMALL QUANTITIES)

This technique is cheaper and less labour intensive than small containers as you don't have to drill holes into lids and zip-lock bags are inexpensive. If a large storage bag is used it will accommodate at least three containers or approximately 100 cockroaches comfortably. This set up consists of the following:

- Place egg/apple cartons into a large storage zip-lock clear bags (27cm by 33cm or greater) that can be purchased from the supermarket (Refer to photo 15).
- Place cut up pieces of carrot at the bottom of the bag
- Make small ventilation holes by stabbing the bag with a sharp circular implement such as a kebab skewer. Avoid knives as they make a long shaped cut which allows cockroaches to escape.
- Using a funnel, pour cockroaches into the bag as shown in photo 9.12.

9.15

Plastic bags don't breathe well, so it is not intended to house cockroaches for long periods and is only suitable for short term transfer.

C) CALICO BAGS (MEDIUM TO LARGE QUANTITIES)

As calico bags breath well, this option is well suited to larger quantities (over 100 cockroaches) and where longer periods of transport are anticipated.

Egg cartons and a small quantity of chopped carrots are placed inside the bag and the top is closed off by twisting a piece of garden twine (Refer to photo 9.16).

9.16

Temporary Storage by Client

The storage methods described above are designed for short term transport and not intended for longer periods. Cockroaches will do much better where they are transferred into a tall, well ventilated storage container as soon as possible after purchase. Another temporary storage option is described in Section 5.5 (Temporary Storage).

As the cockroaches will be stored for a relatively short period prior (as opposed to a permanent breeding colony) the set up can be fairly basic (chopped carrot, and dry food in a small bowl) or any of the option outlined in Chapter 6.0 (Making Food and Water Containers). Given they will be fed to your animals in a matter of days; this is a good opportunity to replace normal dry food with the gut loading recipe in Section 5.4 (Gut Loading and Dusting).

9.4 Economics

Many reptile enthusiasts/wildlife parks spend many thousands of dollars each year feeding their animals. Private individuals and Zoos/wildlife parks can make substantial saving by utilising waste food scraps as a food source for a cricket colony. Unfortunately, due to the high cost of purchasing cockroaches, many people do not provide sufficient live food to their animals.

Estimating the number of reptiles/animals a container supports is variable, and to a large degree is dependent on the cricket consumption chosen by the owner. For instance a person that has the ability to produce large quantities of cockroaches themselves is likely to have a higher cockroach consumption rate (per animal) than someone who purchases them from a pet store at a premium price.

9.0- Grading and Selling

Below are figures that estimate potential savings and cockroach production. Note that the production rate of a container will vary depending on the techniques and materials used, personal skill level, set up (heating systems, maintenance schedule, food quality etc.). The costing's provided below are based on Australian figures (2012), and will need to be adjusted accordingly for other countries and regions.

Cockroach Production from the Waste Wet Food of a Family

The amount of wet food each family produces will vary, however a two adult/two children household could expect to produce sufficient wet food waste (scrap vegetables/fruit) to support approximately 4 large breeding containers. This does not include dry food requirements or the occasional top where household waste wet food consumption is low. Wet food requirements for additional containers will need to be purchased or sourced from your local supermarket (Refer to Chapter 5.0-Food and Water Requirements).

Four Zega Cockroach breeding containers will generally produce approximately 4 standard pet store containers of cockroaches per week. This equates to one pet store container each week for every breeding container.

Small Reptile Collection

A container of cockroaches from the pet store can cost between $6 and $10. Food consumption will vary depending on season and housing setup, however on average an adult bearded dragon will happily consume 1.5 containers in winter and 2.5 containers in summer when there are higher ambient temperatures. This cockroach consumption includes supplementation with fruit/vegetables and includes a day/week fasting. Assuming an average container cost of $7 and an average weekly consumption of 2.0 containers, the owner of an adult bearded dragon could expect to pay approximately $756 per annum.

The production associated from four containers described above, is likely to produce sufficient cockroaches to support two adult bearded dragons on the generous cricket consumption of 2.0 containers per week/animal. This is the equivalent to $1456 per annum. As outlined in the following section, other expenses will need to be considered including dry food and heating costs. Three or four bearded dragons could be supported if a lower cricket consumption rate is chosen (i.e. 1 to 1.5 pet store container of cockroaches/week/bearded dragon).

Larger Private Collections

For financial reasons, many reptile enthusiasts that keep numerous animals have a lower rate of cricket consumption per animal. For instance, some of my clients have advised that the 4 breeding containers described above support approximately 12 medium/large bearded dragons or monitors (30-40cm from tail to snout). This cricket consumption is based on feeding 2-3 days/week feeding cockroaches, 2-3 days per week supplementation with fruit/vegetables/meat (for monitors) and 2 days fasting.

Considerations for Commercial Production

Other people may wish to breed cockroaches for profit. Many wildlife and reptile enthusiasts are always looking for a cheap and fresh supply of food for their animals. This is a great way to turn an expense or unused space at home into an income.

If you do not have time to undertake maintenance of a large colony, consider employing someone where you have sufficient economy of scale and income. Young staff are a cheap and efficient labour source.

Each operation will have a unique set up, location and running costs. It is therefore important to keep good records of costs and income to establish if profits justify further expansion and capital outlay. Below are some tips when starting or incorporating new techniques to existing commercial production:

- Start with a small set up initially to learn the required skills to provide a consistent and reliable product required by commercial clients.
- If you are an existing commercial breeder, trial new techniques before applying them to your whole operation.
- Check with the client on a regular basis that they are satisfied with the product. Live produce can be fickle and can un-expectedly die. Advise your client to contact you if they have received dead stock so they can be replaced. Some people do not wish to raise this issue, so I ask the question on a regular basis to make sure they are receiving healthy stock.
- Keep turning over you stock as frequently as possible. Unsold cockroaches consume food (extra expense to you) and quickly become unsaleable due to higher mortality rates. It is better to get rid of excess stock at a discount, than to retain old stock.

Keep good records of expenses and income to determine if you are making a profit. Below are examples of expenses and income that should be recorded:

Expenses

- Heating costs- electricity and heater purchase costs (Refer to Section 7.3- Reducing Heating Costs, and Section 7.4- Estimating Heating Costs).
- Set up costs including containers, dispensers, container components and shelving
- Consumable items- dry and wet foods, substrate.
- Replacement costs- replacement of gauze in water containers, and new stock required for genetics.
- Depreciation costs- Depreciate the costs of the heat pads/lighting, and containers over a 5-7 year period (adjust as needed). For example a $100 outlay for heat pads and container can be depreciated as a $15/year loss ($100/7 years).
- Travel- costs associated with delivery drop offs and materials pick up.
- Time- Nominate an hourly rate you wish to pay yourself and keep a record of the time taken to do activities (maintenance, sorting, delivery, packaging and selling).
- Wages of employees and yourself.

Income

- Savings made by not having to purchase cockroaches at retail prices.
- Income generated from sales
- Value of materials and goods from bartering (i.e. exchanging cockroaches for reptiles etc.)

9.5 Marketing

Below are some ideas to establish a market for your cockroaches:

- Providing "more cockroaches for less money" and "quality guaranteed" are good philosophies for repeat customers and word of mouth marketing.
- Place an advertisement in the newspaper classified section to obtain commercial and private clients.
- Advertise on electronic and social media's such as E-bay, Twitter, Facebook, Google plus etc. The advantage of social media is that advertising is highly targeted as the advertisements people view have been selected based on their interests (i.e. cricket advertisements would be shown to people with herpetological or wildlife enthusiasts). This concept is taken a step further, with ads now popping up not just on your registered interests, but also general conversation topics. For example if I type in "I was walking my dog today", an advertisement for dog products will appear.
- Pricing may need to be more competitive than the pet store as some clients will need to travel to your premises for pick up. Be as flexible as possible with pick up. If you are not at home when someone wants to pick up the product, you can always leave the cockroaches in a shady spot outside and have the client drop off the money into your letterbox (leave an envelope for this purpose).
- Encourage your clients to give you 24-48 hours' notice prior to pick up to provide sufficient time to sort and package the cockroaches and to organise a pick up time suitable to both yourself and the client.
- Have a variety of cricket packages to suite different clients including small, medium and large orders. Below are some examples of packages which I have found to meet the needs of different clients in Australia. They are examples only and you will need to change the dollar amounts to meet your individual price scheduling.

    1) $4.0 per container (same container content as sold in pet stores, normally between $6-10). All containers have 15% extra than those sold in stores.
    2) 3 small containers (same as sold in pet stores) for $10 is the most popular package sold. This supplies small clients with enough food for approximately 2 weeks. Larger clients can be scaled up to meet their needs (i.e. 6 containers for $20).
    3) Bulk purchases- 1000 cockroaches for $60, which is a common quantity requested by commercial clients.

- Create a flier which clearly outlines pricing schedule, pick up options and advantages of your product over large suppliers (Refer to Appendix 1 for an example flier). This flier can either be dropped off to potential clients or sent out in bulk via email. Follow up potential suppliers with a courtesy phone call to explain your product.

- Potential clients include:
  - Pet owners of reptiles, frogs, arachnids and fish.
  - Wildlife rescue carers who require large quantities of insects insectivorous mammals, birds, reptiles and amphibians
  - Pet stores/animal laboratories, wildlife parks and zoos.
- Try to get bulk purchases from Wildlife parks/pet stores rather than large numbers of small orders. There is a surprisingly large number of herpetological or wildlife rescue enthusiasts who have large herpetological collections which need large volumes of cockroaches on a regular basis. These collectors are well connected and you often get additional customers from word of mouth.
- Potential clients can also be found in smaller satellite centres as they may not have good access to cockroaches or are very expensive due to transport. I have found that remote wildlife parks, pick up cockroaches on their way into town after collecting clients in major centres.
- Contact your local herpetological society, amphibian and native pet group. Place an advertisement in reptile and pet keeping catalogues or magazines.
- Contact your local wildlife rescue group and ask them to send an electronic flier to their members. They will generally be happy to do this as it will give their members access to a cheaper supply of cockroaches.
- Cockroaches and crickets are the main feeder foods for many insectivorous animals. Where possible try to diversify to supply both cockroaches and crickets. Please refer to our webpage (www.zegaenterprises@live.com.au) for details about our low maintenance cricket breeding systems and "The Complete Cricket Breeding Manual".

9.6 Record Keeping

Good record keeping will provide useful information to run the colony more efficiently. The larger the colony the more important it is to keep records to identify containers which need maintenance or harvesting. Below are examples how recording information can help with efficiencies:

- Each container will have a unique food/heating requirement depending on their growth stage. Food requirements rapidly increase when cockroaches transition from medium to large sizes so food amounts will change rapidly at this time. Keeping weekly records will enable you to change food and heating requirements to suit development stage and prevent food waste and fermentation/ hygiene issues.

9.0- Grading and Selling

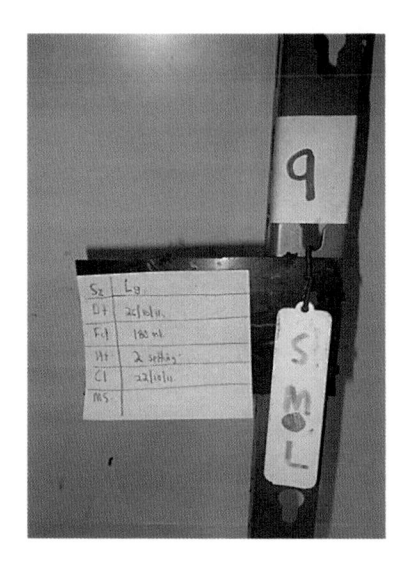

- Quickly determine how much food is required to feed at each feeding session.

- Identifies which containers need cleaning.

Below are examples of how to keep records:

1) Number each container by placing a tag on the lid or on the shelf adjacent to the container. This will enable you to record details in your notebook specific to a container (Refer to photo 9.17).

2) Record information into a note book. Useful information to record includes:

9.17

- Time it takes to clean containers, replace food/water, food preparation, and dispatch cockroaches.
- Electricity consumption and costs (Refer to Section 7.4, Estimating Heating Costs) to establish production costs.
- Ambient temperature of the room/shed where your cockroaches are accommodated over summer and winter (to make sure appropriate temperature ranges are maintained).
- Weight of cockroaches at harvest (i.e. how many grams per thousand)
- Time spent preparing containers/dispensers
- Sales and expenses
- When new genetic stock was added to the breeder container

3) Attach a small piece of paper (stick note pad) onto the lid or onto the shelf next to the container which records the following information required on a regular basis:
- Grams of dry food being consumed at each feed
- Grams of wet food being consumed at each feed
- Heat setting (low, medium, high)

9.0- Grading and Selling

- Date container was cleaned
- Average size of the cockroaches currently

The paper can be attached to the lid by a paperclip which is secured via twine (Refer to photo 9.18). Alternatively the paper can be clipped to a plastic off cut (use plastic cut from the containers when being built) and attached to the shelf with cable ties (Refer to photo 9.17).

9.18

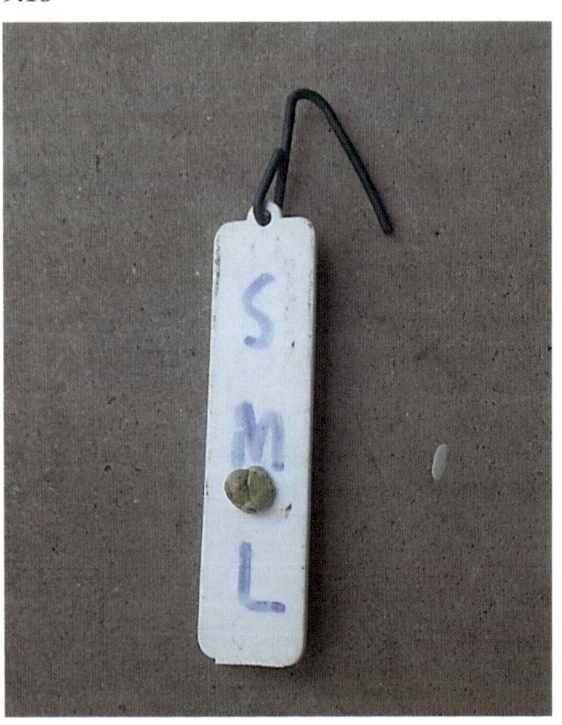

4) Sometimes it is useful to filter a certain size of cockroach and put them into separate containers so each container is a certain size (batch). This makes harvesting the desired cockroach size a lot easier. To distinguish different size categories attach a garden label tag to the frame of the shelf.

5) Attach the tag by bending wire and hooking it to shelving (Refer to photo 9.19). A piece of yellow "stick it" is placed against the letters S, M and L to indicate that this container holds either Small, Medium or Large cockroaches (Refer to photo 9.19).

9.19

The Complete Cockroach Breeding Manual

GLOSSARY

Abdomen	Rear body segment of a cricket that are attached to the back legs.
Ambient	Temperature surrounding an object
Arachnids	Invertebrates with 8 legs including spiders, scorpions, ticks and mites
Carnivorous	Organism with a diet consisting predominantly of animal tissue or material
Cercus	Paired appendages on the rear end of a cockroach
Chitinous	Hard, protective substance found in the exoskeleton of invertebrates.
Compound eye	Eye with thousands of individual photoreceptor units that has a large view angle, and can detect fast movement.
Dry food	Food that have a low water content including pellets, powders, dog and cat food.
Dusting	Process of applying powdered nutrient to a cricket.
Ectothermic	Animals that are unable to generate internal heat, and obtain heat from their external environment (cold blooded).
Exoskeleton	The external skeleton that supports and protects an invertebrates body.
Endothermic	Animals that generate internal heat through metabolism (warm blooded).
Gut loading	High quality food is fed to cockroaches to increase its nutritional content prior to being fed to an animal.
Heat sink	Material which transfers thermal energy from a higher temperature to a lower temperature.
Hydrophobic	Soil which repels water making water absorption difficult.
Invertebrate	An animal without a backbone (e.g. insects, molluscs, crustaceans)
Micro flies	Small flies that can move through normal fly screen.
Metabolism	Chemical reactions which sustain life processes such as growth, repair, and reproduction.
Molting	Shedding exoskeleton or skin as a result of a growth.
Nymphs	Immature form of some insects. A nymph looks very similar to the adult form.
Omnivorous	Organism that has a diet consisting of both animal and plant material

Palps	Elongated appendage near the mouth of an invertebrate, used to explore and help with feeding.
Simple eye	Type of eye which contains a single lens that detects light and movement.
Segmented	The division of an animal's exoskeleton into repeated segments or plates.
Spiracles	Holes located in the exoskeleton of a cricket which allow air to enter the body.
Substrate	Soil or earth
Thorax	Is the middle body segment where the wings and legs attach.
Wet food	Foods that have high water content including vegetables and fruit
Wildlife Rescue	Organizations or individuals who care for injured or orphaned native wildlife

APPENDIX 1- Example Marketing Brochure

More critters for less money!!

Are you disappointed in paying high prices for a container that is half full of dead or dying cockroaches and crickets? We provide both at wholesale prices and guarantee quality

Cockroaches and Crickets Prices

- $4.00 per container (standard container) or……

- 3 containers for $10 or…..

- Bulk buy- 1000 cockroaches for $60

    - We provide 10% more than the standard pet store container.

    - All sizes catered for; large, medium, small and pinhead

    - Fresh and livestock guaranteed at all times.

Bulk purchases

One of the problems of buying crickets in bulk is that they transition from one size to the next within a short period (usually a week or two). This means that within a few weeks they may be larger than required or die if you purchased adults (crickets lifespan is approximately 6 weeks) To overcome this problem, you can purchase 1000 crickets or cockroaches and pick them up in batches of 500. This will ensure that you get the right size cricket for your animals at all times.

One of the advantages of purchasing bulk amounts locally, is that there is no freight costs which can cost nearly as much as the insects.

Pick up

Stock can be picked up from:

- (Insert address) on appointment.

- **Please contact (Insert contact name) on (Insert phone no and email address) to organise purchases.**

Made in the USA
San Bernardino, CA
07 November 2013